COGNITIVE SCIENCE
AND THE
SYMBOLIC OPERATIONS
OF HUMAN
AND ARTIFICIAL
INTELLIGENCE

COGNITIVE SCIENCE AND THE SYMBOLIC OPERATIONS OF HUMAN AND ARTIFICIAL INTELLIGENCE

Theory and Research into the Intellective Processes

Morton Wagman

PRAEGER

Westport, Connecticut
London

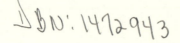

ISBN: 1472943

Library of Congress Cataloging-in-Publicaiton Data

Wagman, Morton.
    Cognitive science and the symbolic operations of human and
artificial intelligence : theory and research into the intellective
processes / Morton Wagman.
       p.   cm.
    Includes bibliographical references and index.
    ISBN 0–275–95853–1 (alk. paper)
    1. Cognition. 2. Cognitive science. 3. Artificial intelligence.
I. Title.
BF311.W26564   1997
153—dc21   96–53618

British Library Cataloguing in Publication Data is available.

Library of Congress Catalog Card Number: 96–53618
ISBN: 0–275–95853–1

First published in 1997

Praeger Publishers, 88 Post Road West, Westport, CT 06881
An imprint of Greenwood Publishing Group, Inc.

Printed in the United States of America

The paper used in this book complies with the
Permanent Paper Standard issued by the National
Information Standards Organizaiton (Z39.48–1984).

10 9 8 7 6 5 4 3 2 1

Contents

Illustrations

FIGURES

Preface

The study of thinking has been undertaken by the disciplines of cognitive psychology and artificial intelligence. Although significant advances have been made, full understanding of the nature of human conceptual thought has yet to be achieved. This book critically examines current theory and research indicative of present status and future promise.

The first chapter of the book focuses on the primary importance of logic and knowledge in cognitive systems. The theoretical foundations of the logical approach to artificial intelligence and the architecture of intelligent agents are examined in depth. The centrality of declarative knowledge and of the predicate calculus is discussed.

The centrality of knowledge in artificial intelligence systems is manifest in the ten-year CYC (from enCYClopedia) research program. CYC, designated to be completed by 1999, will contain an immense knowledge base that comprehensively organizes human knowledge. CYC is systematically compared with logicism and with situated computationalism on a series of foundational issues in artificial intelligence.

The second chapter focuses on significant aspects of human reasoning. Belief-bias effects on logical reasoning and reasoning about causes and enabling conditions is discussed. The probabilistic contrast model of causal reasoning is identified as a significant advance in the development of a mathematical conceptualization of human reasoning.

In the third chapter, analogical thinking, computational and human, is examined in depth. The ARCS (analog retrieval by constraint satisfaction) system uses a parallel constraint satisfaction algorithm to achieve analogical retrieval. Semantic, isomorphic, and pragmatic constraints guide the selection of appropriate analogs for memory. The psychological validity of ARCS and its general applicability are demonstrated. The contribution of ARCS to a general theory of analogical thinking is discussed.

A conceptual component analysis of analogical reasoning is presented. These process components include the recognition of a candidate analogy, the elaboration of analogical mapping, the evaluation of the analogy, and consolidation of the analogy. The sequential process components are applied to a comparative analysis of the strengths and limitations of a number of computational models of analogical thought.

The fourth chapter focuses on the processes of mathematical and scientific discovery in computational and human cognitive systems. Scientific discovery heuristics used at different developmental levels are described. Experimental research in the differential use of effective search heuristics in the space of hypotheses and in the space of experiments is presented in detail, and implications for the philosophy of science are considered.

The fifth and final chapter describes the PAULINE (Planning And Uttering Language In Natural Environments) computer program for pragmatic language generation. The logic, principles, and applications of PAULINE are presented in depth. A critical discussion of the extension of the theoretical and computational concepts embodied in PAULINE to additional areas of language pragmatics concludes the chapter.

Cognitive Science and the Symbolic Operations of Human and Artificial Intelligence is the latest in a series of published and planned volumes that have the consistent theme of developing intellectual grounding for establishing the theoretical and research foundations and the psychological and philosophical implications of a general unified theory of human and artificial intelligence (Wagman, 1991a, 1991b, 1993, 1995, 1996). Each of the volumes contributes important aspects of this enterprise, and each reflects new theory, research, and knowledge in both human and artificial intelligence across the domains of problem solving, reasoning, analogical thinking, learning, memory, linguistic processes, and scientific creativity.

All the volumes are mutually supportive, and all are directed to the same audience: scholars and professionals in psychology, artificial intelligence, and cognitive science. Graduate and advanced undergraduate students in these and related disciplines will also find the book useful.

Acknowledgments

I thank LaDonna Wilson for her assistance in the preparation of all aspects of the manuscript. I am grateful to Steve Wilson for his excellent work in assisting in the preparation of the tables and figures. I am also grateful to Lori Seitz for her excellent typing of portions of the manuscript. I thank Katie Pritchett for her assistance in the preparation of the final draft of the manuscript.

COGNITIVE SCIENCE
AND THE
SYMBOLIC OPERATIONS
OF HUMAN
AND ARTIFICIAL
INTELLIGENCE

1

Artificial Intelligence

THE LOGICAL APPROACH TO ARTIFICIAL INTELLIGENCE

The logical approach to artificial intelligence typically includes the encoding of declarative knowledge in the language of the predicate calculus. The following section describes the theoretical foundation of the logical approach to artificial intelligence.

Logic and Artificial Intelligence: Overview

General aspects of the logical approach to artificial intelligence are discussed in the following account (Nilsson 1991, 31–32):

Until a technical endeavor achieves a substantial number of its goals, several competing approaches are likely to be pursued. So it is with artificial intelligence (AI). AI researchers have programmed a number of demonstration systems that exhibit a fair degree of intelligence in limited domains (and some systems that even have commercial value). However, we are still far from achieving the versatile cognitive skills of humans. And so research continues along a number of paths — each with its ardent proponents. Although successful AI systems of the future will probably draw upon a combination of techniques, it is useful to study different approaches in their pure forms in order to highlight strengths and weaknesses. Here, I present my view of what constitutes the "logical approach" to AI.

Some of the criticisms of the use of logic in AI stem from confusion about what it is that "logicists" claim for their approach. As we shall see, logicism provides a point of view and principles for constructing languages and procedures used by intelligent machines. It certainly does not promise a ready-made apparatus whose handle needs only to be turned to emit intelligence. Indeed, some researchers who might not count themselves among those following a logical approach can arguably be identified with the logicist position. (See, for example, Smith's review of a paper by Lenat and Feigenbaum (1991).) Other, more naive, criticisms claim that since so much human thought is "illogical" (creative, intuitive, etc.), machines based on logic will never achieve human-level cognitive abilities. But puns on the word "logic" are irrelevant for evaluating the use of logic in building intelligent machines; making "illogical" machines is no trouble at all!

In describing logic and AI, we first relate the logical approach to three theses about the role of knowledge in intelligent systems. Then we examine the theoretical foundations underlying the logical approach. For a textbook-length treatment of logic and AI see Genesereth and Nilsson (1987).

The First Thesis: Knowledge of the Environment

The logical approach to artificial intelligence is organized around three general theses, which relate to knowledge of the environment, the centrality of declarative knowledge, and reliance on the predicate calculus. The first thesis is given in the following account (Nilsson 1991, 32):

Thesis 1. Intelligent machines will have knowledge of their environment.

Perhaps this statement is noncontroversial. It is probably definitional. Several authors have discussed what it might mean to ascribe knowledge to machines — even to simple machines such as thermostats (McCarthy, 1979; Rosenschein & Kaelbling, 1986).

The Second Thesis: The Centrality of Declarative Knowledge

In the following section, the salience of declarative knowledge is asserted in the logical approach to artificial intelligence (Nilsson 1991, 32–33, italics added):

Thesis 2. The most versatile intelligent machines will represent much of their knowledge about their environments declaratively.

AI researchers attempt to distinguish between *declarative* and *procedural* knowledge and argue about the merits of each (see, for example, [Hayes, 1977; Winograd, 1975]). Roughly speaking, declarative knowledge is encoded explicitly in the machine in the form of sentences in some language, and procedural knowledge is manifested in programs in the machine. A more precise distinction would have to take into account some notion of *level* of knowledge. For example, a LISP program which is regarded as a program (at one level) is regarded (at a lower level) as a declarative structure that is interpreted by another program. Settling on precise definitions of procedural and declarative knowledge is beyond our scope here. Our thesis simply states that versatile intelligent machines will have (among other things) a place where information about the environment is stored explicitly in the form of sentences. Even though any knowledge that is ascribed to a machine (however represented in the machine) might be given a declarative interpretation by an outside observer, we will not say that the machine possesses declarative knowledge unless such knowledge is actually represented by explicit sentences in the memory of the machine.

When knowledge is represented as declarative sentences, the sentences are manipulated by reasoning processes when the machine is attempting to use that knowledge. Thus, the component that decides how to *use* declarative knowledge is separate from the knowledge itself. With procedural approaches to knowledge representation, knowledge use is inextricably intertwined with knowledge representation.

The first serious proposal for an intelligent system with declarative knowledge was by John McCarthy (1958). McCarthy noted the versatility of declaratively represented knowledge: it could be used by the machine even for purposes unforeseen by the machine's designer, it could more easily be modified than could knowledge embodied in programs, and it facilitated communication between the machine and other machines and humans. As he later wrote, "Sentences can be true in much wider contexts than specific programs can be useful" (McCarthy, 1988).

Smolensky (1988) listed some similar advantages: "a. *Public access*: [Declarative] knowledge is accessible to many people; b. *Reliability*: Different people (or the same person at different times) can reliably check whether conclusions have been validly reached; c. *Formality, bootstrapping, universality*: The inferential operations require very little experience with the domain to which the symbols refer."

To exploit these advantages, the declaratively represented knowledge must, to a large extent, be *context free*. That is, the *meaning* of the sentences expressing the knowledge should depend on the sentences themselves and not on the external content in which the machine finds itself. The context-free requirement would rule out terms such as "here" and "now" whose meaning depends on context. Such terms are called *indexicals*.

Many database systems and expert systems can be said to use declarative knowledge, and the "frames" and "semantic networks" used by several AI programs can be regarded as sets of declarative sentences. On the other hand, there are several examples of systems that do not represent knowledge about the world as declarative sentences.

The Third Thesis: Reliance on Predicate Calculus

The third thesis asserts that an intelligent system represents declarative knowledge in the language of the predicate calculus (Nilsson 1991, 33–34, italics added):

Thesis 3. For the most versatile machine, the language in which declarative knowledge is represented must be at least as expressive as first-order predicate calculus.

One might hope that a natural language such as English might serve as the language in which to represent knowledge for intelligent systems. If this were possible, then all of the knowledge already compiled in books would be immediately available for use by computers. Although humans somehow understand English well enough, it is too ambiguous a representational medium for present-day computers — the meaning of English sentences depends too much on the contexts in which they are uttered and understood.

AI researchers have experimented with a wide variety of languages in which to represent sentences. Some of these languages have limited expressive power. They might not have a means for saying that one or another of two facts is true without saying which fact is true. Some cannot say that a fact is not true without saying what is true instead. They might not be able to say that *all* of the members of a class have a certain property without explicitly listing each of them. Finally, some are not able to state that at least one member of a class has a certain property without stating which member does. *First-order predicate calculus, through its ability to formulate disjunctions, negations, and universally and existentially quantified sentences, does not suffer from these limitations and thus meets our minimal representational requirements.*

The Architecture of Intelligent Agents

A set of concepts is proposed to capture the essential interaction between an intelligent system and the world. Both the system and the world are construed as finite state machines. The mathematical structure of finite state machines is, in the logical approach to artificial intelligence, expressed in the language of the predicate calculus. Details of this very general theory are provided in the following account (Nilsson 1991, 36–38, italics added):

In addition to the three theses just stated, the logical approach to AI also embraces a point of view about what knowledge is, what the world is, how a machine interacts with the world, and the role and extent of special procedures in the design of intelligent machines.

Those designers who would claim that their machines possess declarative knowledge about the world are obliged to say something about what that claim means. The fact that a machine's knowledge base has an expression in it like $(\forall x)Box(x) \supset Green(x)$, for example, doesn't by itself justify the claim that the machine *believes* all boxes are green. (The mnemonic relation constants that we use in our design aren't mnemonic for the machine! We could just as well have written $(\forall x)GO11(x) \supset GO23(x)$.)

There are different views of what it means for a machine possessing a database of sentences to believe the facts intended by those sentences. The view that I favor involves making some (perhaps unusual) metaphysical assumptions about what we take the "real world" to be and about how our machines interact with that world. I will give a simplified account of this view here. It is based, in part, on a discussion of intelligent agent architecture in Genesereth and Nilsson (1987, Chapter 13).

[Figure 1.1] shows a machine interacting with the world. Both machines and world are regarded as finite-state machines. We denote the machine state by M; it is one of a set *M* of states. We denote the world state by W; it is one of a set *W* of states. The input to the machine is denoted by S — one of a set of *S* inputs; the output of the machine is denoted by A — one of a set *A* of outputs. States, inputs, and outputs are related as follows: the function *see* maps W into S; the function *mem* maps S x M into M; the function *act* maps S x M into A; lastly, the function *effect* maps A x W into W. The function *see* models the fact that the machine is not sensitive to every aspect of the world; it partitions the world into classes whose members, as far as the machine is concerned, are equivalent. The function *mem* models the machine's memory behavior; the machine's state at any instant

FIGURE 1.1
Machine and World

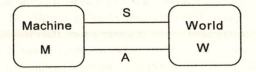

$$see: W \longrightarrow S$$
$$mem: S \times M \longrightarrow M$$
$$act: S \times M \longrightarrow A$$
$$effect: A \times W \longrightarrow W$$

Source: N. J. Nilsson, "Logic and Artificial Intelligence," *Artificial Intelligence* 47 (1989): 31–56. Reprinted with permisison of Elsevier Science Publishers.

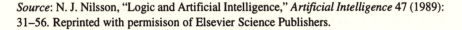

is a function of the machine's input and its previous state. The function *act* describes how the machine acts on the world; its action is a function of its state and its input. We model the effects of these actions on the world (as well as the world's own internal dynamics) by *effect*.

This model of a machine and its world is sufficiently general to capture a number of approaches to intelligent machine design. To particularize it to the logical approach, we stipulate that the state of the machine is given by a set of sentences, which for concreteness we hereinafter take to be sentences in the first-order predicate calculus. The function *mem* transforms such a set of sentences (together with the input to the machine) into another set of sentences (and thus changes the machine's state). The function *act* is a function of such a set of sentences (and the machine's input) and produces as output a machine action.

Describing how the designer specifies *act*, *mem*, and an initial set of sentences requires some discussion about the relationship between these sentences and what the designer imagines the world of the machine to be like. *We suppose that the designer thinks of the world literally as a finite-state machine which he describes as a mathematical structure consisting of objects, functions, and relations.* Some of the objects in this mathematical structure might be states, others might be other entities that the designer thinks exist in the world — some of which are dependent on state. This structure must also account for the finite-state machine function *effect*, which produces a new world state depending on the action of the intelligent machine and the old world state, and the function *see*, which maps world states into the input to the intelligent machine. *AI researchers have explored a variety of ways to conceive of the world in terms of objects, functions, and relations; while we will not describe any particular conceptualization here, they can all be accommodated by the account we are giving. (It may seem strange to think of the real world as a mathematical structure, but since our picture provides for the world to be affected by and affect itself and the intelligent machine, one shouldn't worry that our view of the world is impractically ethereal.)*

Now the designer of a machine that is to interact with the world never knows what the world objects, functions, and relations actually are. He must guess. Guessing involves *invention* on the designer's part. (Our machine designer is in the same predicament as is the scientist; scientists invent descriptions of the world and gradually refine them until they are more useful.) We use the term *conceptualization* to describe the designer's guess about the world objects, functions, and relations. The designer may not even be able to specify a single conceptualization; for example he may choose not to commit himself whether an object he invents, as a block, has the color property green or blue. Thus, in general, the designer attempts to specify a set of conceptualizations such that, whatever the world actually is, he guesses it is a member of the set.

The designer realizes, of course, that his conceptualization might not accurately capture the world — even as he himself believes it to be. For example, his conceptualization may not discriminate between objects that he himself recognizes to be different but which can be considered to be the same considering his purposes for the machine. The designer need only invent a conceptualization that is *good enough*, and when and if it becomes apparent that it is deficient (and that this deficiency is the cause of inadequate machine performance), he can modify his conceptualization.

We stress that the objects guessed to exist in the world by the designer are invented. He is perfectly free to invent anything that makes the machine perform appropriately, and he doesn't ask whether or not some object really does or does not exist (whatever that might mean) apart from these invented structures. For many ordinary, concrete objects such as chairs, houses, people, and so on, we can be reasonably confident that our inventions mirror reality. But some of the things that we might want to include as world objects, such as *precambrian uncon- firmities*, English sentences, *the Peloponnesian War*, π, and *truth*, have a some- what more arbitrary ontological status. In fact, much of the designer's guess about the world may be quite arbitrary in the sense that other guesses would have suited his purposes equally well. (*Even those researchers following other declar- ative, but putatively non-logical, approaches must invent the equivalent of objects, relations, and functions when they attempt to give their machines declar- ative knowledge.*)

A logicist expresses his conceptualization of the world (for the machine) by a set of sentences. The sentences are made part of the machine's memory (com- prising its state) and embody the machine's declarative knowledge. We assume that the sentences are in the first-order predicate calculus; this language and the sentences in it are constructed as follows: For every world object in the concep- tualization we create an *object constant*; for every world relation, we create a *relation constant*; and for every world function, we create a *function constant. Using these constructs, and the syntax of predicate calculus, we (the designer) then compose a set of sentences to express the declarative knowledge that we want the machine to have about the world.*

When a designer cannot (or does not choose to) specify which of two relations holds, he uses a disjunction, such as: $Box(Obl) \wedge [Blue(Obl) \vee Green(Obl)]$. Or he may use an existentially quantified statement: $(\exists x)Box(x) \wedge Green(x)$. Or, he might know that all boxes are green: $(\forall x)Box(x) \supset Green(x)$.

In what sense can we say that a collection of predicate calculus sentences rep- resents *knowledge* about the world? Our answer to this question involves the notions of *interpretations* and *models* of sentences in the predicate calculus. Briefly, an interpretation consists of:

(1) an assignment of a relation to each relation constant;

(2) an assignment of an object to each object constant;

(3) an assignment of a function to each function constant;

(4) a procedure for assigning the values T (true) or F (false) to each closed for- mula. (*This procedure involves evaluating ground atomic formulas using the relation/object/function assignments and then using the standard logical*

truth tables for non-atomic ground sentences. The description of how quantified sentences are evaluated is slightly more complex but respects the intuitive meanings of the quantifiers.)

Any interpretation for which all of the sentences in a set of sentences evaluates to T is called a *model* of the set of sentences.

In terms of these definitions, the designer's task can be re-stated as follows:

Invent world objects, relations, and functions; a first-order predicate calculus language; an interpretation of the expressions of this language in terms of the objects, relations, and functions; and then compose a set of sentences in the language such that the interpretation of those sentences is a model of the set of sentences.

We will call the world objects, relations, and functions invented by the designer, the *intended model* of the sentences the designer uses to describe the world. Although this interpretation itself may never actually be represented explicitly as mathematical structure, it is important that it be firmly fixed in the mind of the designer. With this interpretation in mind, the designer invents linguistic terms to denote his invented objects, functions, and relations and writes down predicate calculus sentences for which the intended interpretation is a model.

The designer gives the machine declarative knowledge about the world by storing these sentences in the machine's memory. We call the set of sentences the *knowledge base* of the machine and denote the set by Δ. We assume that the designer fixes the initial state of the machine by specifying some Δ_0; when the machine is attached to the world, as in [Figure 1.1], *mem* produces a sequence of states $\Delta_0, \Delta_1, ..., \Delta_i, ...$

Even when the designer has a single intended interpretation in mind, Δ, in general, will be satisfied by a set of interpretations — the intended one among them. The designer must provide sufficient sentences in the knowledge base such that its models are limited — limited so that even though the set has more than one model, it doesn't matter given the purposes for the machine. (To the extent that it *does* matter, the designer must then provide more sentences.) In designing knowledge bases, it frequently happens that the designer's idea of intended interpretation is changed and articulated by the very act of writing down (and reasoning with) the sentences.

So, a machine possessing a set of sentences *knows* about the world in the sense that these sentences admit a set of models, and this set is the designer's best approximation to what the world actually is, given the purposes for the machine. The *actual* world might not even be in the set (the designer's guess might be wrong), so we really should be talking about the machine's *beliefs* rather than the machine's *knowledge*. But, following the tradition established by the phrase "knowledge-based systems," we will continue to speak of the machine's knowledge.

The machine's procedural knowledge is represented in the functions *mem* and *act*. The function *mem* changes the sentences and thereby changes the machine's state. Perhaps new sentences are added or existing ones are modified or deleted in response to new sensory information; changes in Δ may occur through processes of deduction or other types of inference as will be described below.

The machine's declarative knowledge affects its actions through the function *act*. We take *act* to be a function (over sets of sentences) that produces actions. Note that *act* can thus only respond to sentences *qua sentences*, that is, as strings of symbols. It is not a function of the models of these sentences!

Given this picture, we can identify a spectrum of design choices. At one end, *act* and *mem* are highly specialized to the tasks the machine is expected to perform and to the environment in which it operates. We might say, in this case, that the machine's knowledge is mainly *procedurally* represented. At the other extreme, *act* and *mem* are general purpose and are largely independent of the application. All application-specific knowledge is represented in Δ. The machine's knowledge in this case can be said to be mainly *declaratively* represented. *The logical approach usually involves a commitment to represent most of the machine's knowledge declaratively. For a proposal at the extreme declarative end, see [Genesereth and Nilsson, 1987, Chapter 13]. It is not yet known to what extent this goal can be achieved while maintaining reasonable efficiency.*

Logical Entailment and Rules of Inference

Reasoning in an intelligent system involves logical entailment formulas and rules of inference, as described in the following account (Nilsson 1991, 38–40):

Among the computations that we might want *mem* to perform are those which add sentences to Δ that are logically entailed by Δ. One apparent problem in devising such computations is the prospect of having to check all the models of Δ to see if they are also models of ϕ. But, fortunately, there exist strictly syntactic operations on Δ that are able to compute logically entailed formulas.

We use the phrase *rule of inference* to refer to any computation on a set of sentences that produces new sentences. If ψ can be derived from Δ by a sequence of applications of rules of inference, we say that ψ can be deduced from Δ and write $\Delta \vdash \psi$. An example is the rule of inference called *modus ponens*. From any sentence of the form $\rho \supset \sigma$ and ρ, we can deduce the sentence σ by modus ponens. The process of logical deduction involves using a set of rules of inference to deduce additional sentences from a set of sentences. Interestingly, it happens that there are rules of inference, modus ponens is an example, that have the property that if $\Delta \vdash \phi$, then $\Delta \models \phi$. Such rules of inference are called *sound*.

Sound rules of inference are extremely important because they allow us to compute sentences that are logically entailed by a set of sentences using computations on the sentences themselves (and not on their models).

We can also find sets of inference rules that have the property that if $\Delta \models \phi$ then the rules (successively applied) will eventually produce a ϕ. Such a set of inference rules is called *complete*.

In summary, intelligent machines designed according to the logical approach are state-machines whose states are sets of sentences. Machine state transitions are governed by a function, *mem*, acting on the sentence sets and the inputs to the machine. An important, but not the only, component of *mem* is sound logical inference. Machine actions are governed by a function, *act*, of the machine's state and inputs. The intended interpretation of the sentences in a machine's state involves objects, functions, and relations that are the designer's guesses about the world.

Through naming comes knowing; we grasp an object, mentally, by giving it a name — hension, prehension, apprehension. And thus through language create a whole world, corresponding to the other world out there. Or we trust that it corresponds. Or perhaps, like a German poet, we cease to care, becoming more concerned with the naming than with the things named; the former becomes more real than the latter. And so in the end the world is lost again. No, the world remains — those unique, particular, incorrigibly individual junipers and sandstone monoliths — and it is we who are lost. Again. Round and round, through the endless labyrinth of thought — the maze (Edward Abbey, 1971, pp. 288–289).

Commentary

Nilsson's view that the world is a mathematical structure has antecedents in the philosophy of Plato and ample demonstration in the achievements of contemporary physical science. Achievements in areas ranging from particle physics to astronomy have depended on the mathematical logic of computers and on programming languages such as the first-order predicate calculus. As Nilsson points out, the first-order predicate calculus is a deductive system independent of context. Lying outside the formal notation of logic, however, are vast areas of human thought and action that are sensitively dependent on context, situation, condition, and nuance. It remains to be seen whether a more powerful logic and language embracing systematic, deductive, noncontextual cognition as well as flexibly adaptive, nondeductive, and context-dependent thinking can be developed to fulfill the dreams of logicism. What would be demanded of such a logic and programming language is an expressive power that captures the reasoning of everyday life: "Life is the art of drawing sufficient conclusions from insufficient premises" (Samuel Butler, as quoted in Kline 1985, 210).

ARTIFICIAL INTELLIGENCE AND THE THRESHOLD OF KNOWLEDGE

In their article, "On the Thresholds of Knowledge," D. B. Lenat and E. A. Feigenbaum (1991) discuss their views on the centrality of knowledge in artificial intelligence systems and describe the comprehensive knowledge system CYC (letters derived from enCYClopedia), a ten-year research project with an expected completion date of 1999.

Knowledge and Artificial Intelligence Research

The following account summarizes an approach to artificial intelligence (Lenat & Feigenbaum 1991, 185):

We articulate the three major findings and hypotheses of AI to date:

(1) *The Knowledge Principle*: If a program is to perform a complex task well, it must know a great deal about the world in which it operates. In the absence of knowledge, all you have left is search and reasoning, and that isn't enough.

(2) *The Breadth Hypothesis*: To behave intelligently in unexpected situations, an agent must be capable of falling back on increasingly general knowledge and analogizing to specific but superficially far-flung knowledge. (This is an extension of the preceding principle.)

(3) *AI as Empirical Inquiry*: Premature mathematization, or focusing on toy problems, washes out details from reality that later turn out to be significant. Thus, we must test our ideas experimentally, *falsifiably*, on large problems.

In the next section, the authors assert that it is primarily knowledge that enables systems (presumably human as well as computer) to exhibit intelligence (Lenat & Feigenbaum 1991, 185–189):

For over three decades, our field has pursued the dream of the computer that competently performs various difficult cognitive tasks. AI has tried many approaches to this goal and accumulated much empirical evidence. The evidence suggests the need for the computer to have and use domain-specific knowledge. We shall begin with our definition of intelligence:

Definition. *Intelligence* is the power to rapidly find an adequate solution in what appears *a priori* (to observers) to be an immense search space.

So, in those same terms, we can summarize the empirical evidence: "Knowledge is Power" or, more cynically "Intelligence is in the eye of the (uninformed) beholder". The *knowledge as power* hypothesis has received so much confirmation that we now assert it as:

Knowledge Principle (KP). A system exhibits intelligent understanding and action at high levels of competence primarily because of the *knowledge* that it can bring to bear: the concepts, facts, representations, methods, models, metaphors, and heuristics about its domain of endeavor.

The word *knowledge* in the KP is important. There is a tradeoff between knowledge and search; that is, often one can either memorize a lot of very detailed cases, or spend time applying very general rules. Neither strategy, carried to extremes, is optimal. On the one hand, *searching* is often costly, compared to the low cost of just not forgetting — of preserving the knowledge for future use. Our technological society would be impossible if everyone had to rediscover everything for themselves. On the other hand, even in a relatively narrow field, it's impractical if not impossible to have a pre-stored database of all the precise situations that one will run into. Some at least moderately general knowledge is needed, rules which can be applied in a variety of circumstances. Since *knowledge* includes control strategies and inference methods, one might ask what is *excluded* by the KP. The answer is that we exclude unbalanced programs: those which do not contain, and draw power from, a mixture of explicit and compiled knowledge, and we advocate programs in which the balance is tipped toward the explicit, declarative side.

Breadth Hypothesis (BH). Intelligent performance often requires the problem solver to fall back on increasingly general knowledge, and/or to analogize the specific knowledge from far-flung domains.

Are we, of all people, advocating the use of weak methods? Yes, but only in the presence of a breadth of knowledge far afield of the particular task at hand. We are adding to the KP here, not contradicting it. Much of the power still derives from a large body of task-specific expertise (cases and rules). We are adding to the KP a new speculation, namely that intelligent problem solvers cope with novel situations by analogizing and by drawing on "common sense".

The natural tendency of any search program is to slow down (often combinatorially explosively) as additional assertions are added and the search space therefore grows. All our real and imagined intelligent systems must, at some level, be *searching* as they locate and apply general rules and as they locate and perform analogical (partial) matches. Is it inevitable, then, that programs must become less intelligent in their previously-competent areas, as their KB's [Knowledge Base] grow? We believe not. The key to avoiding excess search is to have a little meta-knowledge to guide and constrain the search. Hence, the key to preserving effective intelligence of a growing program lies in judicious adding of meta-knowledge along with the addition of object-level knowledge. Some of the meta-knowledge is in the form of meta-rules, and some of it is encoded by the ontology of the KB; these are, respectively, the dynamic and static ways of effectively preserving whatever useful bundlings already existed in the KB. (Of course, meta-rules can and should be represented explicitly, declaratively, as well as having a procedural form. That way, meta-meta-knowledge can apply to *them*; and so on.) This is a prescription for one to gradually add and refine categories and predicates (types of slots) as one grows the KB. This is why we believe the KP works "in the large", why we can scale up a KB to immense size without succumbing to the combinatorial explosion.

Empirical Inquiry Hypothesis (EH). The most profitable way to investigate AI is to embody our hypotheses into programs, and gather data by running the programs. The surprises usually suggest revisions that start the cycle over again. Progress depends on these experiments being able to *falsify* our hypotheses. Falsification is the most common and yet the most crucial of surprises. In particular, these programs must be capable of behavior not expected by the experimenter.

Difficult Problems Hypothesis. There are too many ways to solve simple problems. Raising the level and breadth of competence we demand of a system makes it *easier* to test — and raise — its intelligence.

The Knowledge Principle is a mandate for humanity to concretize the knowledge used in solving hard problems in various fields. This *might* lead to faster training based on explicit knowledge rather than apprenticeships. It has *already* led to thousands of profitable expert systems.

The Breadth Hypothesis is a mandate to spend the resources necessary to construct one immense knowledge base spanning human consensus reality, to serve as scaffolding for specific clusters of expert knowledge.

The Empirical Inquiry Hypothesis is a mandate to actually try to build such systems, rather than theorize about them and about intelligence. AI is a science when we use computers the way Tycho Brahe used the telescope, or Michaelson the interferometer — as a tool for looking at Nature, trying to test some hypothesis, and quite possibly getting rudely surprised by finding out that the hypothesis is false. There is quite a distinction between using a tool to gather data about the world, and using tools to, shall we say, merely fabricate ever more beautiful crystalline scale models of a geocentric universe.

[T]he various principles and hypotheses above combine to suggest a sweeping three-stage research program for the main enterprise of AI research:

(1) Slowly hand-code a large, broad knowledge base.

(2) When enough knowledge is present, it should be faster to acquire more from texts, databases, etc.

(3) To go beyond the frontier of human knowledge, the system will have to rely on learning by discovery, to expand its KB.

Some evidence is then presented that stages (1) and (2) may be accomplished by approximately this century; i.e., that artificial intelligence is within our grasp. Lenat's current work at MCC, on the CYC program, is a serious effort to carry out the first stage by the mid-1990's.

We are betting our professional lives — the few decades of useful research we have left in us — on KP, BH, and EH. That's a scary thought, but one has to place one's bets somewhere, in science. It's especially scary because:

(a) the hypotheses are not obvious to most AI researchers.

(b) they are unpalatable in many ways even to us, their advocates!

Why are they not obvious? Most AI research focuses on very small problems, attacking them with machinery (both hardware and search methods) that over-power them. The end result is a program that "succeeds" with very little knowledge, and so KP, BH, and EH *are irrelevant*. One is led to them only by tackling problems in difficult "real" areas, with the world able to surprise and falsify.

Why are our three hypotheses (KP, BH, EH) not particularly palatable? Because they are unaesthetic! And they entail person-centuries of hard knowledge-entry work. Until we are forced to them, Occam's Razor encourages us to try more elegant solutions, such as training a neutral net "from scratch"; or getting an infant-simulator and then "talking to it". Only as these fail do we turn, unhappily, to the "hand-craft a huge KB" tactic.

The biggest hurdle of all has already been put well behind us: the enormous local maximum of building and using *explicit-knowledge-free* systems. On the far side of that hill we found a much larger payoff, namely expert systems. We have learned how to build intelligent artifacts that perform well, using knowledge, on specialized tasks within narrowly defined domains. An industry has been formed to put this technological understanding to work, and widespread transfer of this technology has been achieved. Many fields are making that transition, from data processing to knowledge processing.

And yet we see expert systems technology, too, as just a local maximum. AI is finally beginning to move beyond that threshold. This paper presents what its authors glimpse on the far side of expert systems local-maximum hill; the promise of a large, broad KB serving as the nucleus of crystallization for programs which respond sensibly to novel situations because they can reason more by analogy than by perfect matching, and, ultimately, because, like us, they understand the meanings of their terms.

The Breadth Principle: Analogical Reasoning

General uses of analogical reasoning are summarized in the following account (Lenat & Feigenbaum 1991, 199):

Analogizing broadens the relevance of the entire knowledge base. It can be used to construct interesting and novel interpretations of situations and data; to retrieve knowledge that has not been stored the way that it is now needed; to guess values for attributes; to suggest methods that just might work; and as a device to help students learn and remember. It can provide access to powerful methods that might work in this case, but which might not otherwise be perceived as "relevant". E.g., Dirac analogized between quantum theory and group theory, and very gingerly brought the group theory results over into physics for the first time, with quite successful results.

Today, we suffer with laborious manual knowledge entry in building expert systems, carefully codifying knowledge and placing it in a data structure. Analogizing may be used in the future not only as an inference method inside a program, but also as an aid to adding new knowledge to it.

CYC and Mapping Human Knowledge

It is possible to anticipate the general time frame and broad strategies required to construct a system that encompasses the realm of human knowledge (Lenat & Feigenbaum, 1991, 209–211):

AI must somehow get to that stage where — as called for by KP and BH — learning begins to accelerate due to the amount already known. Induction will not be an effective means to get to that stage, unfortunately; we shall have to hand-craft that large "seed" KB one piece at a time. In terms of the graph in [Figure 1.2], all the programs that have ever been written, including AM and EURISKO, lie so far toward the left edge of the x-axis that the learning rate is more or less zero. Several of the more successful recent additions to the suite of ML techniques can be interpreted as pushes in the direction of adding more knowledge from which to begin the learning.

The graph in [Figure 1.2] shows learning by induction (DISCOVERY) constantly accelerating: the more one knows, the faster one can discover still more. Once you speak fluently, learning by talking with other people (LANGUAGE) is more efficient than rediscovery, until you cross the frontier of what humanity already knows (the vertical line at x = F), at which point there is no one to tell you the next piece of knowledge.

[Figure 1.2] illustrates two more things. Learning by discovery is much *slower* than other forms of learning — such as being told something in a natural language — but it is the chief method that extends the boundary F of human knowledge.

FIGURE 1.2
The Rate at Which One Can Learn New Knowledge

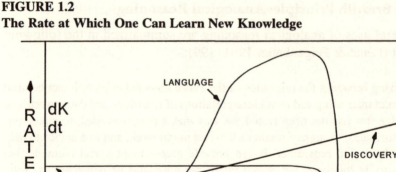

Note: One can also integrate these three curves with respect to time, to see how the total amount known might grow over time.

Source: D. B. Lenat and E. A. Feigenbaum, "On the Thresholds of Knowledge," *Artificial Intelligence* 47 (1991): 185–250. Reprinted with permission of Elsevier Science Publishers.

By contrast, the rate of hand-coding of knowledge is fairly constant, though it, too, drops to zero once we cross the boundary of what is already known by humanity. The hand-coding rate may slope down a bit, since the time to find related concepts will increase perhaps as the log of the size of the KB. Or, instead, the hand-coding rate may slope *up* a bit, since copy and edit is a powerful technique for knowledge entry, and, as the KB grows, there will be more chance that some very similar concept is already present.

This is an example of EH (the Empirical Inquiry Hypothesis . . .): Only by trying to hand-code the KB will we see which of those two counteracting factors outweighs the other, and by how much. Only by continued work on NL and ML will we determine whether or not there is a region, near where all three curves meet, where ML temporarily surpasses NL as a way to grow the KB. And only much further in the future, after our program crosses the frontier F will we find out if the discovery curve begins to slope up or down.

[Figure 1.2] suggests a sweeping three-stage research program for the coming three decades of AI research:

— Slowly hand-code a large knowledge base.

— When enough knowledge is present, it will be faster to acquire more through reading, assimilating databases, etc.

— To go beyond the frontier of human knowledge, the system will have to rely on learning by discovery, carrying out research and development projects to expand its KB.

Three decades: What are the scales on the axes of [Figure 1.2]? Why do we think it's not a three-*century* or three-*millennia* program? Even if the vague shapes of the curves are correct, and even if we are near the left edge, how far over to the right is that place where language understanding meets and then surpasses the hand-coding level? Might we need a trillion things in our knowledge base, in order to get analogy and generalization to pay off? The usefulness and timeliness of the Breadth Hypothesis rest on the following quantitative assumption:

Breadth Is Within Our Grasp. A KB of about a million "frames" will provide a significant performance increase, due to generalization and analogy; this will consume about 2 person-centuries of time, about $50 million, and about 1 decade. Why such a "small size"? That's about all that people know!

Two other ways for bounding the "bits" a human brain can store lead to much larger numbers: (1) counting neurons and synapses; but it's unclear how memories are stored in them; (2) counting pixels in our "mental images"; but controversy rages in cognitive psychology over whether mental imagery is just an illusion caused by the consistency and regularity in the world that lets us fill in missing pieces of memories — and of dynamic sensory experiences — with default values (see, e.g., Fodor & Pylyshyn, 1981). . . . (Also, though it's clearly an oversimplification, having a million entries means that there can be a trillion one-step inferences involving pairs of them. And it would surprise no one to discover that one-step inference is going on unconsciously in our minds constantly.)

Here again is a situation which one could apply to EH. Various theories give various estimates, and the way to settle the issue — and, perhaps, much more importantly, achieve the goal of having the KB we want — is to go off and try to build the large KB. Along the way, it will no doubt become clear how big it is growing and what the actual obstacles are that must be overcome.

In the process of building CYC, a number of surprising research results occur, as described in the following section (Lenat & Feigenbaum 1991, 211–212):

Lenat started the CYC project in late 1984 for this very purpose. It is now halfway through its ten-year time frame, and, most surprisingly, it is still on schedule. A book describing the project and its philosophy has been published [Lenat & Guha 1988], and the interested reader is referred there for details. Here, we shall just very briefly list a few of the surprises that actually trying to build this immense KB has engendered:

(1) The need for more formality, for a more principled representation language. In a typical expert system application, much of the meaning of an entry on a

slot of a frame can be idiosyncratic to that particular application; but CYC, which might be used for any application, cannot afford such sloppiness. E.g., consider placing "IceCream" on the "likes" slot of the "Fred" frame. Does this mean that that's all he likes? Does he like all ice cream? In what sense does he like it? Has he liked it from birth onward (and does it mean he'll like it until he dies), or is there some temporal sub-abstraction of Fred that likes it? etc.

(2) The search for a use-neutral control structure and use-neutral representation is not unlike the search for a single universal carpenter's tool. The pragmatic global *effect* of use-neutrality arises by having a large set of tools that complement each other (and sometimes overlap) and easily work together to get the most common jobs done. On very, very rare occasions, a new tool may have to get invented; use the existing ones to fabricate it then.

(3) In the case of control structure, CYC has by now amassed two dozen separate inference engines: inheritance, inverse slots, automatic classification, Horn clause rules, transfersThrough, etc. One lesson is that it is cost effective to write and fine-tune a separate truth (actually, justification) maintenance system (TMS) for each feature, rather than relying on any one general (but of necessity inefficient) TMS algorithm.

(4) In the case of representation, besides frames, we now have numerous other "tools". One of them is a powerful constraint language which is essentially predicate calculus. This is because much of the knowledge in the system is inherently constraint-like. Consider "The number of children that Joe and Sam have are equal." We could define a new slot sameNumberOfChildrenAs, and such tactics might well get us through any one application, but that's hardly a scalable solution. In general, though, we wanted, needed, and developed a general constraint language. The constraint language is superficially second-order; in almost all real uses, any quantification over predicates (slot names) can be mechanically reduced to first-order. Several dozen of the most common sorts of constraints (e.g., the domain and range of slots) have been "slotized"; i.e., special slots (in this case, makesSenseFor and entry IsA) have been created and optimized, but still the general language is there to fall back on when needed. From time to time, when numerous constraints of the same form have been entered, we "slotize" that form by defining a new slot. For instance, we could create sameNumberOfChildrenAs if there were really heavy use of that sort of constraint.

(5) There are almost ten times as many "frames" required as we had originally expected; luckily, our rate of knowledge entry is also that much faster, so we still hope to "finish" by 1994. In the search for eliminating ambiguity, the knowledge being entered must be more precise than we are used to being in everyday conversation. E.g., the meaning of "Japan" or "water" varies depending on the context of the conversation. Each separate meaning (e.g., political Japan of the 1890s) has its own frame, which is why there are more

than we expected. But balancing that, it is relatively easy to build a knowledge entry tool which assists the user in copying and editing an entire cluster of related frames at once. So the two order-of-magnitude increases are not
unrelated. By the way, "finishing in 1994" means approaching the crossover
point [Figure 1.2], where it will be more cost effective to continue building
CYC's KB by having it read online material, and ask questions about it, than
to continue the sort of manual "brain-surgery" approach we are currently
employing.

CYC and Expert Systems

The problem of integrating hundreds of expert systems as an alternative strategy to that of CYC in attaining a single immense knowledge base
is addressed in the following paragraphs (Lenat & Feigenbaum 1991,
215–218, italics added):

The KP underlies the current explosion of work on expert systems (ESs). Still,
there are additional things our position argues for, that are not yet realized in
today's ESs. Knowledge space *in toto* is not a homogenous solid surface, but
more like a set of self-supporting buttes, and one ought to be able to hop from one
to its neighbors. But current ESs are too narrow, too independent, and too informal, as we discuss below.

One major power source for ESs, the reason they can be so readily constructed, is the synergistic additivity of many rules. Using a blackboard [Erman, Hayes-
Roth, Lesser, & Ready, 1980] or partitioned rule sets, it is possible to combine
small packets of rules into mega-rules: knowledge sources for one large expert
system.

The analogue at the next higher level would be to hook hundreds of large ESs
together, and achieve ever greater synergy. That dream repeatedly fails to mate-
rialize. Why? As we increase the domain of each "element" we are trying to cou-
ple together, the "semantic glue" we need gets to be larger and more sophisti-
cated. The "gluing" or communicating is made all the more difficult by the
unstated and often ambiguous semantics that typically exist in a single ES. We
discussed, earlier, how the CYC project at MCC has been driven toward
increased formality and precision as they have labored to build that large system.
It seems to us that it will require the construction of such a system, as mandated
by the Breadth Hypothesis, and built not haphazardly but with a clean and for-
malized semantics, before the true potential of ES technology will be realized.

Plateau-hopping requires breadth

To harness the power of a large number of disparate expert systems will require
something approaching full consensus reality — the millions of abstractions,

models, facts, rules of thumb, representations, etc., that we all possess and that we assume everyone else does. Moreover, the ESs will need to be coded in a clean, formal representation, and integrated into a global ontology of knowledge. The INTERNIST program is carefully engineered to do a good job of diagnosing diseases from symptoms. But consider coupling it to a machine learning program, which tries to speculate on new disease mechanisms for epidemiology. The knowledge in INTERNIST isn't stored in "the right way", and much of the needed mechanism knowledge has *already* been compiled away, condensed into numeric correlations. Clancey encountered similar difficulties when he tried to adapt MYCIN's diagnostic KB to *teach* medical students [Clancey, 1979].

As we try to combine ESs from various tasks, even somewhat related tasks, their particular simplifications and idiosyncracies prevent synergy. The simplifying was done in the interests of highly efficient and competent problem solving; breadth was not one of the engineering goals.

This naturally results in each ES being a separate, simplified, knowledge universe.

Sometimes the ES's precipitous fall into incompetent behavior is obvious, but sometimes its explanations remain dangerously plausible. Meta-rules about the system's area of competence can guard against this accidental misuse, but that is just a patch. A true solution would be to provide a broad KB so that (1) the plateau sloped off gently on all sides, and (2) we could hop from one ES's plateau or butte to another.

The Local Consistency Hypothesis. There is no need — and probably not even any possibility — of achieving a *global* consistent unification of several expert systems' KBs (or, equivalently, for one very large KB). Large systems need *local consistency*.

The Coherence Hypothesis. Moreover, whenever two large internally consistent chunks C_1, C_2 are similar, their heuristics and analogies should *cohere*; e.g., if the "going up" metaphor usually means "getting better" for C_1, then it should again mean "getting better" for C_2, or else it should not apply at all there.

As regards local consistency, consider how physics advanced for many decades with inconsistent particle and wave models for light. Local consistency is what permits each knowledge-space butte to be independent of the others; as with large office buildings, independent supports should make it easier for the whole structure to weather tremors such as local anomalies. In a locally consistent system, inferring an inconsistency is only slightly more serious than the usual sort of "dead-end" a searcher runs into; the system should be able to back up a bit and continue on. Intelligent behavior derives not from the razor's edge of absolute true verse versus absolute false — from perfect matching — but rather is suggested by plausibility heuristics and supported by empirical evidence.

Coherence is what keeps one from getting disoriented in stepping from one KB butte to its neighbor. Having the metaphors line up coherently can make the hops so small that one is unaware they have hopped at all: "Her academic career, her mood, and her prospects were all going up." See [Lakoff and Johnson, 1980] for many more examples, and a more detailed discussion of this phenomenon. Coherence applies at the conceptual level, not just at the word level. It is not so much the *words* "going up" as the concept, the *script* of moving upwards, that applies coherently in so many situations.

CYC

Overcoming Limitations

In the following section, solutions both to "in principle" limitations and to problems encountered during the construction of CYC are discussed (Lenat & Feigenbaum 1991, 218–220):

Problem 1. *Possible "in-principle" limitations.* There are several extremes that one can point to where the Knowledge Principle and Breadth Hypothesis might be inapplicable or even harmful: perceptual and motor tasks; certain tasks which must be performed in small pieces of real time; tasks that involve things we don't yet know how to represent well (the word "yet" is very important here); tasks for which an adequate algorithm exists; tasks so poorly understood that no one can do it well yet; and (until our proposed large KB becomes reality) tasks involving large amounts of common sense.

Just as we believe that language faculties will require a large consensual reality KB, we expect it to be invaluable in most of the image understanding process (beyond retina-level edge detection and similar operations).

Our response — in principle and in CYC — is to describe perception, emotion, motion, etc., down to some level of detail that enables the system to understand humans doing those things, and/or to be able to reason simply about them. As discussed under Problem 2, below, we let a large body of examples dictate what sorts of knowledge, and to what depth, are required.

A similar answer applies to all the items which we don't yet know very clearly how to represent. In building CYC, e.g., a large amount of effort in the first five years was spent on capturing an adequate body of knowledge (including representations and problem-solving strategies) for time, space, belief, substances, and so on. We did not set out to do this, the effort was driven completely empirically, completely by need, as we examined snippets of encyclopedia and newspaper articles and had to develop machinery to represent them and answer questions about them. Our response is a tactical hypothesis, not a strategic one; we would find it interesting if it is falsified, but the effect would be negligible on our overall research strategy.

Tasks which can be done without knowledge, or which require some that no one yet possesses, should be shied away from. One does not use a hammer to type with.

This research opportunity is finally being pursued; but until CYC or a similar project succeeds, the knowledge-based approach must shy away from tasks that involve a great deal of wide-ranging common sense or analogy.

Problem 2. *How exactly do we get the knowledge?* Knowledge must be extracted from people, from databases, from the intelligent systems' KBs themselves (e.g., thinking up new analogies), and from Nature directly. Each source of knowledge requires its own special extraction methods.

In the case of the CYC project, the goal is to capture the full breadth of human knowledge. To drive the acquisition task, Lenat and his team examine pieces of text (chosen from encyclopediae, newspapers, advertisements, and so on), sentence by sentence. They aren't just entering the facts as stated, but — much more importantly — are encoding what the writer of that sentence already knew about the world. These are the facts and heuristics and simplified models of the world which one would need in order to understand the sentence, things which should be insulting or confusing for the writer to have actually stated explicitly (e.g., if coke is commercially consumed to turn ore into metal, then coke and ore must both be worth less than metal). They also generalize each of these as much as possible (e.g., the products of commercial processes are more valuable than their inputs). Another useful place they focus is the inter-sentential gap; in a historical article, what actions should the reader infer have happened between each sentence and the next one? Yet another focus: what questions should anyone be able to answer having just read that article? These foci drive the extraction process. Eventually, CYC itself began helping to add knowledge, by proposing analogues, extending existing analogies, and noticing gaps in nearly symmetric structures.

Problem 3. *How do we adequately represent it?* Human experts choose or devise representations that enable the significant features of the problem to remain distinguished, for the relevant connections to be quickly found, etc. Thus, one can reduce this to a special case of Problem 2, and try to elicit appropriate representations from human experts. CYC takes a pragmatic approach: when something proves awkward to represent, add new kinds of slots to make it compactly representable. In extreme cases, add a whole new representation language to the toolkit. Besides frames and "rules" and our formal constraint language (described above), we use stored images and neural nets as representation schemes. Images are useful for users to point at; e.g., to say something about the strike plate of a door lock — if you don't happen to know what it's called, but you could pick it out instantly given a photo of a door lock. Statistical space partitioning (neural nets) may be useful for certain kinds of user modeling (e.g., gesture level), and the CYC group is currently training one on examples of good analogizing, so as to suggest promising "hunches" of new analogies to investigate, an activity which CYC will then do symbolically.

The quality of the solutions to many of these "Problems", including this one, depend on the quality of our system's emerging ontology. What category boundaries are drawn; what individuals get explicitly represented; what is the vocabulary of predicates (slots) with which to describe and interrelate them, etc.? Much of the 1984–89 work on CYC has been to get an adequate global ontology; i.e., has been worrying about ways to represent knowledge; most of the 1990–94 work will be actually representing knowledge, entering it into CYC. That is why we have "only" a million entries of CYC's KB today, but expect dozens of times that many in 1994.

Guiding Principles

The basic principles underlying the CYC research project are summarized in the following account (Lenat & Feigenbaum 1991, 223–224):

Our position includes the statements:

— One must include *domain-specific* knowledge to solve difficult problems effectively.

— One must also include both *very general* knowledge (to fall back on) and very *wide-ranging* knowledge (to analogize to), to cope with novel situations.

— We already have plenty of theories about mechanisms of intelligence; we need to proceed empirically: go off and build large testbeds for performing, analogizing, ML, NL.

— Despite the progress in learning, language understanding, and other areas of AI, *hand-crafting* is still the fastest way to get the knowledge into the program for at least the next several years.

— With a large KB of facts, heuristics, and methods, the fastest way will, after some years, tip toward NL (reading online textual material), and then eventually toward ML (learning by discovery).

— The hand-crafting and language-based learning phases may each take about one decade, partially overlapping (ending in 1994 and 2001, respectively, although the second stage never quite "ends"), culminating in a system with human-level breadth and depth of knowledge.

Each of those statements is more strongly believed than the one following it. There is overwhelming evidence for the KP and EH. There is strong evidence in favor of the BH. There is a moderate basis for our three-stage program. And there is suggestive evidence that it may be possible to carry out the programs this century.

Social Implications

The social implications of CYC and artificial intelligence, more generally, are discussed in the following section (Lenat & Feigenbaum 1991, 224–225, italics added):

The impact of systems mandated by the KP and BH cannot be overestimated. Public education, e.g., is predicated on the *un*availability of an intelligent, competent tutor for each individual for each hour of their life. AI will change that. Our present entertainment industry is built largely on passive viewing; AI will turn "viewers" into "doers". What will happen to society as the cost of wisdom declines, and society routinely applies the best of what it knows? Will a *knowledge utility* arise, like an electric utility, and how might it (and other AI infrastructures) effect [*sic*] what will be economically affordable for personal use?

When we give talks on expert systems, on commonsense reasoning, or on AI in general, we are often asked about the ethical issues involved, the *mental* "environmental impact" it will have, so to speak, as well as the direct ways it will alter everyday life. We believe that this technology is the analogue of language. We cannot hold AI back any more than primitive man could have suppressed the spread of speaking. It is too powerful a technology for that. Language marks the start of what we think of as civilization; we look back on pre-linguistic cultures as uncivilized, as comprised of intelligent apes but not really human beings yet. Can we even imagine what it was like when people couldn't talk to each other? Minsky recently quipped that a century from now people might look back on us and wonder "Can you imagine when they used to have libraries where the books didn't talk to each other?" Our distant descendants may look back on the synergistic man-machine systems that emerge from AI, as the natural dividing line between "real human beings" and "animals". We stand, at the end of the 1980's, at the interstice between the first era of intelligent systems (competent, thanks to the KP, but quite brittle and incombinable) and the second era, the era in which the Breadth Hypothesis will finally come into play.

Man-Machine Synergy Prediction. *In that "second era" of knowledge systems, the "system" will be reconceptualized as a kind of colleagular relationship between intelligent computer agents and intelligent people. Each will perform the tasks that he/she/it does best, and the intelligence of the system will be an emergent of the collaboration.*

The interaction may be sufficiently seamless and natural that it will hardly matter to anyone which skills, which knowledge, and which ideas resided where (in the head of the person or the knowledge structures of the computer). It would be inaccurate to identify Intelligence, then, as being "in the program". From such man-machine systems will emerge intelligence and competence surpassing the unaided human's. Beyond that threshold, in turn, lie wonders which we (as unaided humans) literally cannot today imagine.

Commentary

The greatest challenge for the CYC project is not the efficient organization of immense amounts of knowledge. A truly advanced intelligence must include a deep, self-heightened comprehension of its own electronic information.

SHRDLU, ELIZA, PARRY, and other automata rely for any sense they make on the human users who project their full understanding and allowance onto an ignorant, limited artifice that uses words but does not understand what the words mean — a situation analogous to that of the compact disc player that cannot understand what it is that it is performing that we recognize and appreciate as the violin trio.

Regarding SHRDLU, ELIZA, PARRY, MYCIN, MACSYMA, and DENDRAL, among others, none of these "artificial intelligences" understand what they are "talking" about. They use words to parrot, or as children aged six or seven might be taught to say "E=MC^2" or, indeed, as college students can repeat a formula in mathematics or physics but cannot put into their own words the meaning(s) of the mathematical symbols.

In their "intelligent" interactions with human beings, SHRDLU does not know what blocks are, ELIZA does not know what psychotherapy clients are, PARRY does not know what psychiatrists are, MACSYMA does not know what mathematicians are, MYCIN does not know what physicians are, and DENDRAL does not know what chemists are.

Humans project human knowledge onto machines just as they project advanced knowledge onto children who recite "E=MC^2" or "Vanity, all is vanity." Through a more advanced education, children gain increased knowledge of what they are talking about; gradually, their understanding deepens and widens so that they can use mathematical symbols and literary phrases with the specific nuances required in given contexts.

Even if humans could educate and develop the machines' artificial intelligence, there would be no point to doing so. Machines have been designed for their automatic functions: to perform symbolic operations, to perform services, to save humans from repetitious tasks, and to protect humans from mechanical errors. Human designers provide machines with only the minimum conditions necessary for them to perform as mechanical intellectual servants — that is, to perform intellectual tasks as opposed to a physical task such as plowing.

In addition to the necessary conditions, however, humans do not bestow upon machines the sufficient conditions involving knowledge of what the machines are doing and judgments about when that knowledge renders the products of the machines valid.

And yet, paradoxically and poignantly, the automatic functions that computers achieve for us may result — in the case of the most intellectual of disciplines, mathematics — in a desperate or laughable situation, in which computers achieve mathematical proofs for us and cavalierly assert that humans are incapable of comprehending these proofs. The following account is noteworthy (Horgan 1993, 103):

Ronald L. Graham of AT&T Bell Laboratories suggests that the trend away from short, clear, conventional proofs that are beyond reasonable doubt may be inevitable. "The things you can prove may be just tiny islands, exceptions, compared to the vast sea of results that cannot be proved by human thought alone," he explains. Mathematicians become increasingly dependent on experiments, probabilistic proofs and other guides. "You may not be able to provide proofs in a classical sense," Graham says.

Of course, mathematics may yield fewer aesthetic satisfactions as investigators become more dependent on computers. "It would be very discouraging," Graham remarks, "if somewhere down the line you could ask a computer if the Reimann hypothesis is correct and it said, 'Yes, it is true, but you won't be able to understand the proof.'"

Traditionalists no doubt shudder at the thought.

ARTIFICIAL INTELLIGENCE AND THE ELECTRIC ENCYCLOPEDIA

In the following section, Smith (1991) analyzes the CYC research project (Lenat & Feigenbaum 1991). The analysis compares the Lenat and Feigenbaum position with the position of logicism and embedded computationalism on a set of 12 foundational issues in artificial intelligence.

General Critique of the Lenat and Feigenbaum Position

The article "The owl and the electric encyclopedia" reviews a conceptual and research proposal for the development of an immense knowledge system that would capture all of human intelligence and eventually surpass it (Smith 1991, 251–253, italics added):

The original version of Lenat and Feigenbaum's paper (the one presented at the Foundations of AI conference, in response to which this review was initially written) was considerably more optimistic than the revision published here some four years later. *For one thing, their estimate of the project's scale has grown: whereas in 1987 they suggested the number of things we know to be many hundreds of thousands — perhaps a few million — that estimate has now increased to many millions (perhaps a few hundred million). In addition, whereas their original paper suggested that inference was essentially a non-problem (a sentiment still discernable in their "Knowledge Is All There Is Hypothesis," p. 192), the project is now claimed to incorporate at least two dozen separate inference engines, with more on the way.* Again, not only has the sophistication of their representation scheme increased, but . . . their representational conventions have developed from those of a simple frame system towards something much more like full predicate calculus, complete with propositions, constraints, set-theoretic models, etc. (Their words: "the need for more formality, for a more principled representation language" was one of the "surprises that actually trying to build this immense KB has engendered.") All these signs of increased sobriety are reassuring, of course, although, given their ambition and eclecticism, one wonders whether the resulting complexity will be manageable.

More seriously, a conceptual shift has overtaken the project — more ramifying than these relatively simpler issues of scale. At the 1988 CYC review meeting (in Palo Alto), Lenat claimed that whereas he and Feigenbaum had initially taken their project as one of coding up everything in the encyclopedia (hence the name "CYC"), they were now convinced that the real task was to write down the *complement* of the encyclopedia: everything we know, but have never needed to say. This is an astounding reversal. Dreyfus (1981) should feel vindicated, since this shift in focus certainly strengthens any doubts about the ultimate adequacy of an allegiance to explicit representation.

For all that, their optimism remains intact. *They still believe that by 1994 they will approach the crossover point where a system will pass the point of needing any further design or hands-on implementation, and will from then on improve simply by reading and asking questions (implying, I suppose, that AI's theoretical preliminaries will be concluded). Furthermore, they suggest that this second "language-based learning" stage will in turn end by about the end of the decade, at which point we will have a system "with human-level breadth and depth of knowledge."* They claim these things, furthermore, in spite of such telling admissions as the following, written in 1989: "much of the 1984–89 work has been to get an adequate global ontology; i.e., has been worrying about ways to represent knowledge; most of the 1990–94 work will be actually representing knowledge, entering it into CYC." In their present paper, Lenat and Feigenbaum take up the enthusiast's cause, defending a new flavour of "great expectation." *They suggest that just a million frames, massaged by already-understood control structures, could intelligently manifest the sum total of human knowledge.*

Lenat and Feigenbaum (L&F) announce their own impressive generalizations: the Knowledge Principle, the Breadth Hypothesis, the Empirical Inquiry Hypothesis, etc. Each, in its own way, makes sense: that competence in a domain arises because of specific knowledge of the constitutive subject matter; that "intelligent performance often requires the problem solver to fall back on increasingly general knowledge, and/or to analogize to specific knowledge from far-flung domains"; etc. I agree; I expect most readers would agree. . . . *The problem is that L&F, with only the briefest of intervening discussion, then arrive at radically concrete claims, such as that three decades will suffice to carry out the following sweeping three-stage research program: (i) the slow hand-coding of a frame-based knowledge base, approximating "the full breadth of human knowledge" ($50 million, due to be completed by 1994), sufficient to bring the system to a point (ii) where it will be able to read and assimilate the remaining stage material on its own (approximately the turn of the century), followed by a stage (iii) where it is forced to carry out its own program of research and discovery, since it will have advanced "beyond the frontier of human knowledge."*

One is reminded of tunnel diodes. For a moment the argument is on the plane of common sense, and then — presto! — it is suddenly at an extreme level of specificity, without ever having been anywhere in between. *From the generality of human knowledge to the intricacies of slot inheritance; from the full flowering of intelligence to particular kinds of controlled search — leaps like these are taken without warning, often mid-sentence. The problem is not simply that the reader may disagree with the conclusions, but that there is no hint of the complex intellectual issues and decades of debate that lie in the middle. I.e., whereas tunneling electrons — or so we're told — genuinely switch from one place to another without ever being half-way in between, arguments don't have this luxury. Truth and reason are classical, so far as we know, constrained to follow continuous trajectories. That's why the middle ground of conceptual analysis and carefully laid-out details is the stuff and substance of AI.*

So: After giving a better sense (in the next section) of the sort of argument that's missing, I will take it as the task of this review to map out at least some of the intermediate conceptual territory. The immediate goal will be to figure out what view of its structure could have led L&F to tunnel through in the way they did. As for their conclusions, I've already suggested I find them implausible, but others will want to judge for themselves. My larger aim is to convince the reader that any serious assessment of L&F's paper (or indeed of analogous proposal) must be made against the backdrop of that hidden middle realm.

Comparing Positions on 12 Foundational Issues

In the following section, a set of 12 central foundational issues is proposed in terms of which the Lenat and Feigenbaum position can be evaluated (Smith 1991, 259–260):

We're brought right back to where we started: with that hidden middle realm. Let's dig deeper, therefore, and uncover some of its inner structure. I'll do this by locating L&F's position with respect to twelve foundational questions — questions that could be asked of any proposed reasoning or inference system. Given that we lack a general theory of representation (not only those of us in AI, but the wider intellectual community as well — a sobering fact, since our systems rest on it so fundamentally), posing such questions is as good an analytic strategy as any. Furthermore, these twelve will help reveal L&F's representational assumptions.

The answers are summarized in [Table 1.1]. To convey a better sense of the structure of the territory, I've flanked L&F's position with two other replies. On the left is the position of traditional formal logic (the system studied by philosophers and logicians, not "logic-based" theorem provers or programming language — both too ill-defined to be of much help here). On the right is my own assessment of the minimum an AI system will require in order to achieve anything like genuine intelligence. For discussion, I'll call it a notion of "embedded computation" (EC).

TABLE 1.1
A Dozen Foundational Questions

	Logic	L & F	EC
1. Primary focus on explicit representation?	yes	yes	no
2. Contextual (situated) content?	no	no	yes
3. Meaning dependent on use?	no	no	yes
4. Consistency mandated?	yes	no	no
5. Single representational scheme?	yes	yes	no
6. Entirely discrete (no continuity, images, . . .)?	yes	yes	no
7. Representation captures all that matters?	yes	yes	no
8. Reasoning and inference central?	yes	yes	yes
9. Participation and action crucial?	no	no	yes
10. Physical embodiment important?	no	no	yes
11. Support for "original" semantics?	no	no	yes
12. Distinguish theorist's and agent's conceptual schemes?	no	no	yes

Source: B. C. Smith, "The owl and the electric encyclopedia," *Artificial Intelligence 47* (1991): 251–288. Reprinted with permission of Elsevier Science Publishers.

One point needs emphasizing, before turning to specifics. Embedded computation is still an emerging perspective, not yet a technical proposal. That doesn't make it sheer speculation, however, nor is it purely idiosyncratic. A growing number of researchers (Agre, 1985, 1989; Brooks, 1986; Kaelbling, 1987; Winograd & Flores, 1986) are rallying around similar views — so many, in fact, that one wonders whether something like it won't be the next AI stage, beyond the "explicit knowledge" phase that L&F represent. Nonetheless, I would be the first to admit that details remain to be worked out. But that's exactly my point. I'm contrasting it with L&F's position exactly in order to highlight how far I believe we are from achieving their stated goals. For purposes of the present argument, in other words, any claim that we don't yet understand some aspect of the speculative EC view — what nondiscrete computation would be like, say — counts *for* my position, and *against* L&F. All that matters is that there is some reason to believe that the issue or phenomenon in question is at least partially constitutive of intelligence. L&F are the ones with the short-term timetable, after all, not I.

Explicit Representation

The following section compares the centrality of explicitness in representing knowledge in the conceptual positions of Lenat and Feigenbaum, logic, and embedded computationalism (Smith 1991, 260–262).

Question 1. Does the system focus primarily on the explicit representation?

(	Logic	L&F	EC)
(	yes	yes	no)

In the current design of computer systems, there is probably no more time-worn technique than that of "explicit representation." And there is no difficulty in discerning L&F's views on the subject, either. They line up directly with tradition. In fact, that representation be explicit is the only specific coding requirement they lay down (it is mandated in their "Explicit Knowledge Principle"). Similarly, the CYC project takes explicit representation as its fundamental goal.

Unfortunately, however, it is unclear what L&F (or anyone else, for that matter) mean by this term — what, that is, the implicit/explicit distinction comes to (see Kirsh [1990] for a recent paper on the notion). This is not to say that the notion doesn't matter. Many programmers (and I count myself as one of them) would stubbornly insist that choices about explicit representation impinge on effectiveness, control flow, and overall system architecture. The question is what that insistence is about.

When pressed for examples of explicit representation, people typically point to such cases as the grammarian's "S → NP VP," logical formulae such as "P(a) ⊃ Q(b)," frames in such systems as KRL, or nodes in semantic nets. The examples are almost always taken from language-like representational schemes, suggesting that some combination is required of conceptual categorization, recursive method of combination, and relative autonomy of representational element (images and continuous representations are rarely, though not never, cited as paradigmatically explicit). Explicitness is also relational, holding between something (a representation) and something else (what it represents). This provides some freedom: a given structure can be implicit, explicit, neither (if, like a breadbasket, it doesn't represent anything), or both (if it represents severally). Logical axioms, for example, are often viewed as explicit representations of their own particular contents, but (in ways that Levesque [1984], Fagin and Halpern [1985], and others have tried to make precise) as implicit representations of what they imply.

So what does explicitness come to? Though it's currently impossible to say, it seems to require a roughly determinate object (sentence, frame, whatever), of a readily discriminable type, that simultaneously plays two rather direct roles: straightforwardly representing some content or other (John's having brown hair, say), and, again quite directly, playing a causal role in the course of the system's life that constitutes that system's knowing or believing the corresponding content (or would at least lead an observer to say that the system knows or believes it). I.e., explicitness seems to require (a) a degree of modularity or autonomy, (b) a coincidence of semantic and causal role, and (c) a relative directness or immediacy of the latter.

In contrast, people would label as *implicit* the representation of the letter "A" in a run-length encoded bitmap representation of a page of text, or the representation of the approach velocity of an oncoming car in the frequency difference between the outgoing and incoming radar signals in a police speed trap, or (as suggested above) the representation of a fact by the explicit representation of a different set of facts, when the first is a distant entailment of the latter set. In each case the representational element is either itself relationally encoded, or else one of its two "consequent" relations, instead of being direct, is in turn complex and relational; between the structure and its content, or between the structure and the inferential role relevant to that content.

Assuming this reconstruction points in even roughly the right direction, let's go back to L&F. To start with, it makes sense of why L&F contrast explicit with "compiled" representations (since compilation often removes the structural autonomy of distinct source elements), and of their assumption that facts can be represented in relative independence: simple content and simple causal consequence, neither depending much on what else is represented, or how anything else is used. As will become clearer in a moment, this theme of modularity, directness, and relative independence characterizes L&F's proposal at a variety of levels. (I'm prepared to argue that L&F's proposal won't work, but I'm not claiming it doesn't have a degree of integrity.)

What about the flanking views? At the level of whole systems, formal logic is paradigmatically explicit (in spite of the "implicit" treatment of entailment mentioned above — what matters is that the explicit representations are the ones that are theoretically analyzed). If forced at theoretical gun-point to produce an "explicit representation" of the structure of Abelian groups, for example, it's hard to imagine a better place to start than with first-order axiomatization. And yet, in part as indicated by their repeated desire for a relatively minimal role for deduction and complex reasoning (see Question 8, below), L&F are even more committed to explicit representation than adherents of logic. That is to endorse a very serious amount of explicitness indeed.

The embedded view? It would be hard to argue that explicitness representation isn't powerful, but, as discussions of the next questions will suggest, it carries a price of potentially unwarranted definiteness, premature categorization, and resistance to some sorts of recognition. My main dispute, however, isn't over its utility. Rather, I question whether, if explicit representation is indeed an identifiable subspecies (the only construal on which it could matter at all), it is the only sort that's required. That is something I wouldn't want to admit without a lot more evidence. In particular, I worry that a system comprised only of explicit representations would be fatally disconnected from the world its representations are about. (For analogous views, . . . see the exploratory systems of Rosenschein & Kaelbling [1987], Brooks [1986], and Chapman & Agre [1987], and the writings of Suchman [1986], Cussins [1990], Dreyfus [1979], and Smolensky [1988].)

L&F may of course reply that they do embrace implicit representation, in the form of compiled code, neural nets, and unparsed images. But this isn't strictly fair. By "the L&F position" I don't mean the CYC system per se, in inevitably idiosyncratic detail, but rather the general organizing principles they propose, the foundational position they occupy, the theoretical contributions they make. I.e., it isn't sufficient to claim that the actual CYC software does involve this or that embedded aspect, as, in many cases, I believe it *must*, in order to work at all. . . . Rather, my plaint is with overarching intellectual stance.

Representation Context

The following section examines the role of context in intelligibility and in intelligent systems (Smith 1991, 262–264, italics added):

Question 2. Is representational content contextual (situated)?

(Logic	L&F	EC)
(no	no	yes)

Under the general rubric of the term "situated" ("situated language" [Barwise & Perry, 1983], "situated action" [Suchman, 1986], "situated automata" [Rosenschein & Kaelbling, 1987]) a variety of people have recently argued that adequate theory cannot ignore the crucial role that context plays in determining the reference and semantic import of virtually all linguistic and other intentional phenomena. Context is obviously important in interpreting "now," "tomorrow," and "it's raining"; and in determining the temporal implications of tense. In its full glory, however, the situated claim goes much deeper: that you can't ultimately understand anything except as located in the circumstances in which it occurs.

Here's a way to say it: the sum total of facts relevant to the semantical valuation of a system's representational structures (i.e., the relevant context) will always outstrip the sum total of facts that that system represents (i.e., its content).

What, then, of the three proposals under review? Traditional logic, again paradigmatically, ignores context. The logical viewpoint, to use a phrase of Nagel's (1986), embodies the historical imagination's closest approximation yet to a "view from nowhere." Contextual influence isn't completely gone, of course — it still plays a role in assigning properties and relations to predicates, for example, in selecting the "intended interpretation." But as far as possible logical theories ignore that ineliminable residue.

L&F are like the logicians: they ignore context too. And they have to. Context isn't a simple thing — something they don't happen to talk about much, but could add in, using their touted mechanism for coping with representational inadequacy: namely, adding another slot. On the contrary, their insistence that their "knowledge base" project can proceed without concern as to time, place, or even kind of use, is essentially an endorsement of a-contextual representation.

For my part (i.e., from the embedded perspective), I think the situated school is on to something. Something important. Even at its most objective, intelligence should be viewed as a "view from somewhere" (Smith, in press). Take an almost limiting case: suppose you were to ask L&F's system how many years it would be before the world's population reached 7 billion people? Without a contextual grounding for the present tense, it would have no way to answer, because it wouldn't know what time it was. L&F might reply by claiming they could easily add the "current date" to their system, and tie in arithmetic procedures to accommodate "within 10 years." My responses are three: *(i) that to treat the particular case in this ad hoc way won't generalize; (ii) that this repair practice falls outside the very foundational assumptions on which the integrity of the rest of their representational project is founded; and (iii) that the problem it attempts to solve absolutely permeates the entire scope of human knowledge and intelligence.*

Meaning and Use

The following section elaborates on the role of context in order to demonstrate independence of meaning on use (Smith 1991, 264–267, italics added):

Question 3. Does meaning depend on use?

(Logic	L&F	EC)
(no	no	yes)

This question gets at a much more radical claim than the last. The idea is not only that content or final interpretation of a representational structure (sentence, frame, whatever) depends on the situation in which it is used, but that what the structure means can't be separated from the whole complex of inferential, conversational, social, and other purposes to which it is put. . . . Still, use-dependent meaning does pose problems for a theorist. Take just two examples. First, it undermines the very coherence of the notion of sound (or complete) inference; those concepts make sense only if the semantic values of representational formulae are conceptually independent of their role in reasoning. The problem isn't just that there is no obvious model-theoretic analysis, since it is unclear what model-theoretic structure would be assigned to the term "water." Or even, setting model theory aside, that it is unclear what a well-defined semantical value for such a term could be. More seriously, soundness is fundamentally a claim that the use of a term or predicate has respected its independently given semantical value. Making interpretation dependent on use, at least at first blush, therefore gives one every reason to suppose that the notion of soundness is rendered circular, hence vacuous.

Second, it is a likely consequence of this view that the meaning or significance of a complex representational structure won't be able to be derived, systematically, from the "bottom up," but will instead have to be arrived at in some more holistic way. It challenges, in other words, the traditional view that semantics can be "compositionally" defined on top of a base set of atomic value. I.e., the point isn't just that the interpretation of a sentence (its propositional value) is sometimes determined by mutually interlocking constraints established by various sentential constituents (as suggested in indexical cases, such as for the pronoun structure in "though Jim didn't like her, Mary was perfectly happy with him"), say by some sort of relaxation method. Rather, a deeper claim is being made: that the very meaning of the parts of a discourse can depend on the interpretation of the whole. And if it is whole sentences that connect with situations, this may have to be done not bottom-up in terms of the representational constituents, but if anything top-down.

None of this suggests that representation, or interpretation, is impossible. What it does bring into question are the assumptions on which such a system should be built, including for example the inferential viability of a system without any access to the interpretation of its representational structures — without, that is to say, *participating* in the subject matters about which it *reasons* (one way in which to resolve the obvious difficulty raised by the statement just made: that an agent know what is being said other than through the vehicle of the saying). But I'll leave some of these speculations until a later question.

For the time being, note merely that logic avoids this "meaning-depends-on-use" possibility like the plague. In fact the "use = representation + inference" aphorism reflects exactly the opposite theoretical bias: that representation (hence meaning) is an independent module in the intentional whole.

Once again, L&F's position is similar: nothing in their paper suggests they are prepared to make this radical a move. At one point they do acknowledge a tremendous richness in lexical significance, but after claiming this is all metaphor (which typically implies there is a firm "base case"), they go on to assert, without argument, that "these layers of analogy and metaphor eventually 'bottom out' at physical — somatic — primitives: up, down, forward, back, pain, cold, inside, seeing, sleeping, tasting, growing, containing, moving, making noise, hearing, birth, death, strain, exhaustion. . . ." It's not a list I would want to have responsibility for completing.

More seriously, the integrity of L&F's project *depends* on avoiding use-dependent meaning, for the simple reason that they don't intend to consider use (their words: "you can never be sure in advance how the knowledge already in the system is going to be used, or added to, in the future," which they take as leading directly to the claim that it must be represented explicitly). If we were to take the meaning-depends-on-use stance seriously, we would be forced to conclude that *nothing in their knowledge base means anything*, since no one has yet developed a theory of its use.

I.e., L&F *can't* say yes to this one; it would pull the rug out from under their entire project.

In contrast (and as expected), the embedded view embraces the possibility. Perhaps the best way to describe the tension is in terms of method. A liberal logicist might admit that, in natural language, meaning is sometimes use-dependent in the ways described, but he or she would go on to claim that proper scientific method requires idealizing away from such recalcitrant messiness. My response? That such idealization throws the baby out with the bathwater. *Scientific idealization is worth nothing if in the process it obliterates the essential texture of what one hopes to understand. And it is simply my experience that much of the structure of argument and discourse — even, the raison d'être of rationality — involves negotiating in an intentional space where meanings are left fluid by our linguistic and conceptual schemes, ready to be grounded in experience.*

The Problem with Consistency

The necessity of consistency in the positions of Lenat and Feigenbaum, logic, and embedded computation is discussed in the following account (Smith 1991, 267–269):

Question 4. Is consistency mandated?

(Logic	L&F	EC)
(yes	no	no)

L&F are quite explicit in rejecting an absolute dependence on consistency, to which traditional logical systems are so famously vulnerable. As indicated in the table [above], this is the first of the dozen questions where they and the embedded view align. That much said, however, it's not clear how deep the similarity goes. In particular, I'm unsure how much solace can be found in their recommendation that one carve the "knowledge base" into separate "buttes," and require each to be locally consistent, with neighbouring buttes maximally coherent. At least it's not clear, once again, without a much better intermediate theory.

Fundamentally, the problem is that consistency is a relational property — the consistency of a set of sentences stands or falls on the set as a whole, not on an individual basis. This means that some relations between or among sentences (or frames) will have to be used as a basis for the partition (and to tie the resulting "buttes" together). Call these the system's *organizational principles*. Without them (or any remotely reasonable assumptions of error rates, dependence, etc.) the number of possible different configurations meeting their structural requirements would be intractably immense.

Furthermore, the organizational principles can't themselves be defined in terms of consistency; organizing a database *by* internal consistency would be crazy. Rather, I take it that what L&F really want is to be able to demonstrate (local) consistency for a database organized according to some other metric. What other metric? Surely only one makes sense: according to similarity or integrity of subject matter. *X* should be stored next to *Y*, in other words, because of the presence of (semantic) compatibility, not just the absence of (syntactic) incompatibility. Otherwise, descriptions of national politics might nestle up to lists of lemon meringue pie ingredients, but be kept separated from other statements about Washington policy making — so that things ended up together not because they agreed, but because they didn't have anything to do with one another.

So adequate organization will need to be defined in terms of a notion of subject matter. But where are we to find a theory of that? The problem is similar to that of representation in general: no one has one. The issue comes up in natural language attempts to identify topic, focus, etc. in theories of discourse (see, e.g., Grosz & Sidner [1986]), and in some of the semantic work in situation theory (Barwise, 1986; Barwise & Etchemendy, 1989). But these are at best a start. Logic famously ducks the question. And informal attempts aren't promising: if my experience with the KRL project can be taken as illustrative (Bobrow, Winograd et al., 1977), the dominant result of any such attempt is to be impressed with how seamlessly everything seems to relate to everything else.

When all is said and done, in other words, it is unclear how L&F plan to group, relate, and index their frames. They don't say, of course, and (in this case) no implicit principles can be inferred. But the answer is going to matter a lot — and not just in order to avoid inconsistency, but for a host of other reasons as well, including search, control strategy, and driving their "analogy" mechanism. Conclusion? That viable indexing (a daunting problem for any project remotely like L&F's), though different from consistency, is every bit as much in need as anything else of "middle-realm" analysis.

And as for consistency itself, we can summarize things as follows. Logic depends on it. L&F retain it locally, but reject it globally, without proposing a workable basis for their "partitioning" proposal. As for the embedded view . . . the standard notion of consistency doesn't survive its answer to Question 3 (about use-dependent meaning). That doesn't mean, however, that I won't have to replace it with something analogous. In particular, I have no doubt that *some* notion of semantic viability, integrity, respect for the fact that the world (not the representation) holds the weight — something like that will be required for any palatable intentional system. Important as contextual setting may be, no amount of "use," reasoning processes, or consensual agreement can rescue a speaker from the potential of being wrong. More seriously, I believe that what is required are global *coordination conditions* — conditions that relate thinking, action, perception, the passing of the world, etc., in something of an indissoluble whole. To say more now, however — especially to assume that logic's notion can be incrementally extended, for example, by being locally proscribed — would be to engage in tunneling of my own (but see Smith [in press]).

Representational Schemes

The following section discusses the dependence of general intelligence on multiple representational schemes (Smith 1991, 269–271):

Question 5. Does the system use a single representational scheme?

(Logic	L&F	EC)
(yes	yes	no)

Tucked into a short paragraph of L&F's Section 9 is their response to the charge that one might encounter representational difficulties in trying to capture all of human knowledge. Their strategy is simple: "When something proves awkward to represent, add new kinds of slots to make it compactly representable." In fact they apparently now have over 5000 kinds. If only representation were so simple.

Several issues are involved. To start with, there is the question of the expressive adequacy of their chosen representational system — frames, slots, and values.

Especially in advance, I see no reason to believe (nor argument to convince me) that mass nouns, plurals, or images should succumb to this scheme in any straightforward way — or, to turn it upside down, to suppose that, if an adequate solution were worked out within a frame-and-slot framework, that the framework would contribute much to the essence of the solution. Frames aren't rendered adequate, after all, by encoding other representational schemes within them. As indicated in their current comments, L&F have apparently expanded their representational repertoire in recent years. Instead of relying solely on frames and slots, they now embrace, among other things: blocks of compiled code, "unparsed" digitized images, and statistical neural networks. But the remarks made in this section still largely hold, primarily because no mention is made of how these different varieties are integrated into a coherent whole. The challenge — still unmet in my opinion — is how the "contents" contained in a diverse set of representational schemes are semantically commensurable, in such a way as to support a generalized, multi-modal notion of inference, perception, judgment, and action. For some initial work in this direction see Barwise & Etchemendy (in press) for general introduction, and Barwise & Etchemendy (1990) for technical details.

Furthermore, one wonders whether any single representational framework — roughly, a representation system with a single structural grammar and interpretation scheme — will prove sufficient for all the different kinds of representation an intelligent agent will need. Issues range from the tie-in to motor and perceptual processing (early vision doesn't seem to be frame-like, for example; is late vision?) to the seeming conflict between verbal, imagistic, and other flavours of memory and imagination. You might view the difficulties of describing familiar faces in words, or of drawing pictures of plots or reductio arguments, as problems of externalizing a single, coherent, mentalese, but I suspect they really indicate that genuine intelligence depends on multiple representations, in spite of the obvious difficulties of cross-representational translation.

Against all such considerations, however, logic and L&F are once again similar in pledging allegiance to a single representational scheme. As representative of the embedded view, I'll vote for variety.

Discrete and Continuous Representations

The following section discusses whether discrete representation is sufficient for all varieties of intelligence (Smith 1991, 271–272):

Question 6. Are there only discrete propositions (no continuous representation, images . . .)?

(Logic	L&F	EC)
(yes	yes	no)

If pressed to represent continuous phenomena, L&F would presumably entertain real numbers as slot values, but that barely scratches the surface of the differences between discrete representations like formulae in a formal language, and various easily imagined forms of continuity, vagueness, indeterminacy, analogues, etc. And it is not just that we can imagine them; anything like real intelligence will have to deal with phenomena like this. We have the whole messy world to capture, not just the distilled, crystalline structure of Platonic mathematics.

In assessing the typology of representation, the distinction between discrete (digital) and continuous (analogue) representations is sometimes given pride of place, as if that were the ultimate division, with all other possibilities subcategorized below it. But other just as fundamental divisions cross-cut this admittedly important one. For example, there is a question of whether a representation rests on a conception or set of formulated categories, or is in some way pre- or non-conceptual (terminology from Cussins [1990]). The natural tendency, probably because of the prevalence of written language, is to assume that discrete goes with conceptual, continuous with non-conceptual, but this isn't true. The use of ocean buoys to demarcate treacherous water, for example, is presumably discrete but non-conceptual; intonation patterns to adjust the meaning of words ("what an *extraordinary* outfit") are at least plausibly both continuous and conceptual. Or consider another distinction: whether the base or "ur-elements" on which a representation is founded have determined edges or boundaries. Both discrete and continuous objects of the sort studied in mathematics (the integers, the real line, and even Gaussian distributions and probability densities) are determinate, in the sense that questions about them have determinate answers. It's unclear, however, in questions about when tea-time ends, or about what adolescence is, or about exactly how many clouds there were when you poked your head out of your tent and said, with complete confidence, "there are lots of clouds today" — it's unclear in such cases whether there are determinate answers at all. The problem isn't an epistemic one, about incomplete knowledge, or a linguistic one, about the exact meanings of words. The point is that the metaphysical facts just aren't there — nor is there any reason to suppose they should be there — to support a clean, black-and-white distinction. The competent use of the English plural, that is to say, doesn't require the existence of a denumerable base set of discrete elements. I am convinced that this distinction between phenomena that have sharp boundaries (support determinate answers) and those that don't is more profound and more consequential for AI than the distinction between discrete and continuous instances of each variety.

Modern logic, needless to say, doesn't deal with foundational indeterminacy. Nor are we given any reason to suppose that L&F want to take it on. One wonders, however, whether our lack of understanding of how relative certainty can arise on top of a foundationally vague base (no one would deny that there were lots of clouds outside that tent, after all) may not be the most important obstacle to the development of systems that aren't brittle in the way that even L&F admit we're limited to today.

Representation and Full Situation Significance

The following section argues that representations do not completely capture the significance of situations (Smith 1991, 272–275):

Question 7. Do the representations capture all that matters?

(Logic	L&F	EC)
(yes	yes	no)

The situated view of representation cited earlier rests on the tenet that language, information, and representation "bridge the gap" . . . between the state of the user(s) of the representation, and the state of the world being referred to. It's a position that accords with a familiar view of language as dynamic action, rather than simply as static description. And it has among its more extreme consequences the realization that not all of what matters about a situation need be captured, at least in the traditional sense, in the meanings of its constituent representations.

However, I intend with this seventh question to get a stronger position yet: that the full significance of an intentional action (not just a communicative one) can crucially involve *non-representational* phenomena, as well as representational ones. I.e., it is a claim that the millenial story about intelligence won't consist solely of a story about representation, but will inevitably weave that story together with analyses of other, non-representational aspects of an intentional agent. Some of these other ingredient stories will describe salient facts of embodiment (possibly even including adrenaline levels), but they will talk about other things as well, including genuine *participation* in represented subject matters, and the internal *manifestation* (rather than *representation*) of intentionally important properties. Some modern roboticists, for example, argue that action results primarily from the dynamical properties of the body; the representational burden to be shouldered by the "mind," as it were, may consist only of adjustments or tunings to those non-representational capacities (see, e.g., Raibert [1986]; Raibert and Sutherland [1983]). Rhythm may similarly as much be exhibited as encoded in the intelligent response to music.

How do our three players stand on this issue? I take it as obvious that L&F require what logic assumes: that representation has to capture all that matters, for the simple reason that there isn't anything else around. For L&F, in other words, facts that can't be described might as well not be true. . . . They are forced to operate under a maxim of "inexpressible → irrelevant."

In contrast, as I've already indicated, I take seriously the fact that we are beaten up by the world — and not only in intentional ways. I see no reason to assume that the net result of our structural coupling to our environment — even that part of that coupling salient to intelligent deliberation — is exhausted by its representational record. And if that is so, then it seems overwhelmingly likely that the full structure of intelligence will rely on that residue of maturation and embodiment. So I'll claim no less for an embedded computer.

Here's a way to put it. L&F believe that intelligence can rest entirely on the meaning of *representations*, without any need for correlated, *non-representational experience*. On the other hand, L&F might also imagine their system starting to read and distill things on its own. What will happen, however, if the writers tacitly rely on non-representational actions on the part of the reader? The imagined system wouldn't be able to understand what it was reading.

The Essentiality of Inferential Processes

The evidential importance of inferential processes in formal and practical reasoning is discussed in the following section (Smith 1991, 275–277):

Question 8. Are reasoning and inference central?

(Logic   L&F   EC   )

(yes   yes   no   )

When logicians develop axiomatic accounts of set theory, criteria of elegance and parsimony push towards a minimal number of axioms — typically on the order of a dozen — from which an infinite number of truths follow. It's a general truth: economy of statement is often a hallmark of penetrating insight.

No one, however, expects distilled scientific theories alone to sustain complete, workaday, general-purpose reasoning. It is obvious that any reasonable problem solver (like any imaginable person), rather than deriving all its conclusions from first principles, will depend on a rich stock of facts and heuristics, derived results and rules of thumb — to say nothing of a mass of a-theoretic but relevant particulars (such as who it's talking to). So we should expect general intelligence to rest on a relatively high ratio of relevant truths to foundational axioms, especially in the face of resource-bounded processing, complex or just plain messy subject matters, and other departures from theoretical purity.

Nonetheless, you can't literally know everything. No matter how knowledgeable, an agent will still have to think in order to deal with the world *specifically* — to conclude that if today is Tuesday then tomorrow must be Wednesday, for example (derived from the general fact that Wednesdays follow Tuesdays), or to figure out whether your friend can walk from Boston to Cambridge, not otherwise having heard of your friend. Universal instantiation and modus ponens may not be all there is to thought, but without some such faculty a system would be certifiably CPU-dead. And instantiating universals is only the beginning. "Inference"

includes not only deduction, but induction, abduction, inference to the best explanation, concept formation, hypothesis testing — even sheer speculation and creative flights of fancy.

It shouldn't be surprising, then, that inference is the one issue on which all
three positions coincide — logic, L&F, and EC. But superficial agreement
doesn't imply deep uniformity. There are questions, in each case, as to what that
commitment means.

A collection of inferential schemata are provided — each demonstrably truth-
preserving (the first requirement), and each applicable to an indefinite set of sentences (the second). But, as AI knows so well, something is still missing: the
higher-level strategies and organizational principles necessary to knit these atomic steps together into an appropriate rational pattern. Being able to reason, that is
to say, isn't just the ability to take the right atomic steps; it means knowing how
to think creatively about the world. Traditional logic, of course, doesn't address
these questions. Nor — and this is the important point — is there any a priori reason to believe that that larger inferential demand can be fully met within the con-
fines of logic's peculiar formal and semantic conventions.

On the other hand — and this takes us to the embedded view — once one
moves beyond logic's familiar representational assumptions (explicit, a-contextual representation, and so forth), no one has yet presented an inferential model
that meets the first demand. To accept the embedded answers to Questions 1–7 is
thus to take on a substantial piece of homework: developing, from the ground up,
a semantically coordinated and rationally justifiable notion of inference itself.
This is just one of the reasons why the embedded perspective is still emerging.

What about L&F? They have two options. To the extent that they agree with
the present characterization of their position, vis-à-vis Questions 1–7, they would
probably want to avail themselves of logic's notion of inference. For reasons discussed earlier, however, this isn't enough: they would still have to take a stand
on the relationship between truth-preserving logical entailment and the appropriate structure of rational belief revision, . . . to say nothing of providing a finite
account of an appropriate set of high-level control strategies, in order to provide
a complete answer to the second demand. On the other hand, to the extent that
they feel confined by logic's stringent representational restrictions (as they admit
they do, for example, at least with respect to its insistence on full consistency —
see Question 4), and want to embrace something more like the embedded view,
then they too must answer to the much larger demand: of not simply presenting
their inferential mechanism (let alone claiming to have embraced 20 different
ones), but of explaining what their very notion of inference is.

Coordination of Reasoning and Action

The effective coordination of thought and action is discussed in the following section (Smith 1991, 278–279):

Question 9. Are participation and action crucial?

(Logic   L&F   EC)

(	no	no	yes)

Reasoning is a form of action. Earlier I commented on L&F's relegation of reasoning to a secondary status by their treatment of it as search, their suggestion that the "control" problem is largely solved, and their claim that with enough "knowledge" deep reasoning will be largely unnecessary.

But reasoning isn't the only kind of action that (at least in humans) has to be coordinated with representation. . . . Representations that lead to action often have to be revised in light of that very action's being taken.

Coordination management, as I will call this indissoluble blend of adjustment, feedback, action, belief revision, perception, dance, etc., arises in many corners of AI, ranging from planning and robotics to systems dealing with their own internal state (reflection and meta-level reasoning). Nor is AI the first discipline to recognize its importance: philosophers of science, and theorists of so-called "practical reasoning," have always realized the importance — and difficulty — of connecting thinking and doing. Students of perception, too, and of robotics, wrestle with their own versions of the coordination problem.

So we end this one with a curious tally. In virtue of its utterly disconnected stance, and of *not being a computational system*, logic is singularly able to ignore action and subject matter participation. On the embedded side, I take participatory connections with the world as not just important, but as essential. In fact the embedded view could almost be summed up in the following claim:

Participation in the subject matter is partially constitutive of intelligence.

When all is said and done, in other words, I believe the term "intelligent" should be predicated on an integrated way of being that includes both thought and action, not simply an abstract species of disconnected symbol manipulation. This may contravene current theoretical assumptions, but I suspect it is consonant with ordinary common sense. Frankly, I don't see how you could believe a system could comprehend all of consensus reality without being able to understand "See you tomorrow!".

Between these two, L&F occupy a somewhat unstable middle ground. I have listed them with logic, since that's where their claims go; there is no hint that they envisage tackling issues of coordination. On the other hand, they will have to confront coordination management merely in order to get their system to turn over, quite apart from whether it manifests anything I would call intelligence.

Physical Substrate and Theoretical Computation

The following section argues that a complete account of intelligence must include the physical substrate of computation and representation (Smith 1991, 279–281):

Question 10. Is physical embodiment important?

(Logic	L&F	EC)
(no	no	yes)

The authors of the mathematical theory of computability claimed as a great victory their elevation of the subject of computation from messy details of physical implementation and fallible mechanism onto a pure and abstract plane. And the prime results of recursive function theory, including the famous proofs of undecidability, genuinely didn't seem to rely on any such implementational details. Modern programmers don't typically traffic in recursive function theory in any very conscious way, but they still accept the legacy of a computational level of analysis separate from (and possibly not even theoretically reducible to) the physical level at which one understands the underlying physical substrate.

More recently, however, especially with the increasing realization that relative computability is as important as (if not more important than) the absolute computability of the 1930s, the story is growing murkier. Though it treats its subject matter abstractly, complexity theory still deals with something called time and space; it's not entirely clear what relation those rather abstract notions bear to the space and time of everyday experience (or even to those of physics). At least with regard to time, though, real (non-abstract) temporal properties of computation are obviously important. Whether differences among algorithms are measured in minutes, milliseconds, or abstract "unit operations," the time they take when they run is the same stuff that I spend over lunch. And the true spatial arrangement of integrated circuits — not just an abstracted notion of space — plays an increasing role in determining architectures.

Although it isn't clear where this will all lead, it does allow the question to be framed of whether considerations of physical embodiment impinge on the analysis of a given computational system. For traditional logic, of course, the answer is *no*; it is as pure an exemplar as anything of the abstract view of computation and representation. And once again L&F's stance is similar: nothing suggests that they, along with most of the formal tradition, won't ignore such issues.

Again the embedded view is different. I am prepared to argue that physical constraints enter computational thinking in a variety of familiar places. For one thing, I have come to believe that what (in a positive vein) we call the "formality" of computation — the claim, for example, that proof procedures rely solely on the formal properties of the expressions they manipulate — amounts in the end to neither more nor less than "whatever can be physically realized in a causally efficacious manner." But this is not the only place where physical realization casts its shadow. Consider one other example: the notion of locality that separates doubly-linked lists from more common singly-linked ones, or that distinguishes object-oriented from function-based programming languages. Locality, fundamentally, is a physical notion, having to do with genuine metric proximity. The question is whether the computational use is just a metaphor, or whether the "local access" that a pointer can provide into an array is metaphysically dependent on the locality of the underlying physics. As won't surprise anyone, the embedded viewpoint endorses the latter possibility.

The Authenticity of Computer Semantics

The philosophical and communicative implications of accepting or rejecting original semantics in computers is discussed in the following passage (Smith 1991, 281–282):

Question 11. Does the system support "original" semantics?

(Logic	L&F	EC)
(no	no	yes)

It has often been pointed out that books and encyclopedias derive their semantics or connection to what they're about from the people that use them. The analogous question can be asked about computers: whether the interpretations of the symbol structures they use are in any sense "authentic" or "original" to the computers themselves, or whether computational states have their significance only through human attribution (see, e.g., Dennett [1987]; Haugeland [1981]; Searle [1981]).

The question is widely accepted, but no one has proposed a really good theory of what is required for semantical originality, so not a whole lot more can be said. Still, some of the themes working their way through this whole set of questions suggest that this issue of originality may be relevant not only for philosophical reasons but also for purposes of adequate inference and reasoning. In particular, if the only full-blooded connection to subject matter is through external users, then it follows that a system won't be able to avail itself of that connection in carrying out its processes of symbol manipulation, reasoning, or inference. If, on the other hand, the semantic connection is autonomous (as one can at least imagine it is, for example, for a network mail system that not only represents facts about network traffic, but also sends and receives real mail), then the chances of legitimate inference may go up.

So the question should be read as one of whether the way of looking at the system, in each case, points towards a future in which systems begin to "own" their semantic interpretations — if still in a clunky and limited way, then at least with a kind of proto-originality.

Even that vague a formulation is sufficient to corral the votes — and to produce another instance of what is emerging as the recurring pattern. Like logic, L&F neither address nor imagine their system possessing anything like the wherewithal to give its frames and slots autonomous referential connection with the world. In fact something quite else suggests itself. Given the paucity of inference they imagine, the heavy demands on indexing schemes, and the apparent restriction of interaction to console events, L&F's system is liable to resemble nothing so much as an electric encyclopedia. No wonder its semantics will be derivative.

Now it's possible, of course, that we might actually want an electric encyclopedia. In fact it might be a project worth pursuing — though it would require a major and revealing revision of both goals and procedure. Note that L&F, on the current design, retain only the formal data structures they generate, discarding the natural language articles, digests, etc., used in its preparation. Suppose, instead, they were to retain all those English entries, thick with connotation and ineffable significance, *and use their data structures and inference engines as an active indexing scheme.* Forget intelligence completely, in other words; take the project as one of constructing the world's largest hypertext system, with CYC functioning as a radically improved (and active) counterpart for the Dewey decimal system. Such a system might facilitate what numerous projects are struggling to implement: reliable, content-based searching and indexing schemes for massive textual databases. CYC's inference schemes would facilitate the retrieval of articles on related topics, or on the target subject matter using different vocabulary. And note, too, that it would exploit many current AI techniques, especially those of the "explicit representation" school.

But L&F wouldn't be satisfied; they want their system itself to know what those articles mean, not simply to aid us humans. And it is against that original intention that the embedded view stands out in such stark contrast. With respect to owls, for example, an embedded system is more likely to resemble the creatures themselves than the *Britannica* article describing them. And this, I submit, to return to the question we started with, is the direction in which semantical originality lies.

Representational Differences in the Designer and in the System

The significance of ultimate discrepancies in the representational capacities of the system and its designer is discussed in the following account (Smith 1991, 282–284):

Question 12. Is room made for a divergence between the representational capacities of theorist and agent?

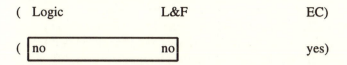

(Logic	L&F	EC)
(no	no	yes)

The final question has to do with the relation between the representational capacities of a system under investigation, and the typically much more sophisticated capacities of its designer or theorist. I'll get at this somewhat indirectly, through what I'll call the *aspectual* nature of representation.

Computers, however, generally don't possess anything remotely like our discriminatory capacities, and as a result, it is a very substantial question for us to know how (from their point of view) they are representing the world as being. For example (and this partly explains [D. V.] McDermott's [1981] worries about the wishful use of names), the fact that we use English words to name a computer system's representational structures doesn't imply that the resulting structure represents the world for the computer in the same way as that name represents it for us.

I suspect that the lure of L&F's project depends in part on their ignoring "as" questions, and failing to distinguish theorists' and agents' conceptual schemes. Or at least this can be said: that they are explicitly committed to not making a distinction between the two. In fact quite the opposite is presumably their aim: what they want, of the system they propose to build, is something that we can interact with, in our own language (English), in order to learn or shore up or extend our own understanding of the world. In order for such interaction to work — and it is entirely representational interaction, of course — the two conceptual schemes will have to be commensurable, on pain of foundering on miscommunication.

Here, though, is the problem. I assume (and would be prepared to argue) that an agent (human or machine) can only carry on an intelligent conversation using words that represent the world in ways that are part of that agent's representational prowess. For an example, consider the plight of a spy. No matter how carefully you try to train such a person to use a term of high-energy physics, or the language of international diplomacy, subsequent conversations with genuine experts are almost sure to be awkward and "unintelligent" (and the spy therefore caught!) unless the spy can genuinely come to register the world in the way that competent users of that word represent the world as being.

It follows, then, that L&F's project depends for its success on the consonance of its and our conceptual schemes. Given that, the natural question to ask is whether the sketch they present of its construction will give it that capacity. Personally, I doubt it, because, like [G.] Evans (1982) I am convinced that most common words take their aspectual nature not only from their "hook-up" to other words, but from their direct experiential grounding in what they are about. And, as many of the earlier questions have indicated, L&F quite clearly don't intend to give their system that kind of anchoring.

So once again we end up with the standard pattern. Neither traditional logic nor L&F take up such issues, presuming instead on what may be an unwarranted belief of similarity. It is characteristic of the embedded view to take the opposite tack; I don't think we'll ever escape from surprises and charges of brittleness until we take seriously the fact that our systems represent the world differently from us.

Commentary

Smith concludes his long analysis with a summarizing statement from the poet W. B. Yeats: "Man can embody the truth, but cannot know it." This is fine poetry but hardly modern science.

In advocating the position of situated computationalism, B. C. Smith is critical of both the logicist approach and the explicit knowledge-intensive approach of D. B. Lenat and E. A. Feigenbaum. Representation for Smith is "implicit, contextual, and embodied" (1991, 285). It would be more accurate to view cognition in humans and computers as both explicit and implicit, both declarative and procedural, both automatic and strategic. What is learned may be learned explicitly, but with repeated performance automaticity takes over. Now the cognitive strategy is implicit, proceduralized and, Smith would say, "embodied" (1991, 285).

In addition, a functioning intelligence, human or computer, requires knowledge that is general and specific, reasoning that is exact and fuzzy, heuristics that are specialized and generalized. A full account of intelligence requires not separated contending positions but judiciously unified viewpoints.

2

Reasoning

BELIEF-BIAS AND LOGICAL REASONING

Validity and Truth in Logic

It is important that research in the psychology of logical reasoning follows the principles of logic that govern the complex relationships between the validity-invalidity of arguments and the truth-falsity of premises and conclusions. Invalid argument patterns can consist of true premises and true conclusions, true premises and false conclusions, false premises and true conclusions, or false premises and false conclusions. Valid argument patterns can consist of true premises and true conclusions, false premises and true conclusions, or false premises and false conclusions. The pattern of valid arguments, true premises, and false conclusions is not extant in the principles of logic.

Experiment in Belief-Bias and Logical Reasoning

Overview

The research of H. Markovits and G. Nantel is summarized in the following account (1989, 11):

In this study, we examined whether adult subjects' beliefs regarding the empirical truth of a conclusion affected their production as well as their evaluation of a logical conclusion in a reasoning task. In addition, the relation between the ability to resolve an abstract reasoning problem correctly and the effect of belief-bias was examined. The subjects were given one of four paper-and-pencil reasoning tasks, two of them using an evaluation paradigm, and two of them using a production paradigm. Each paradigm comprised either neutral problems or belief problems. The neutral problems were constructed to be as similar as possible to the belief problems in order to control for extraneous factors. All four tasks also included an abstract reasoning problem. The results indicate a significant belief-bias effect for both the evaluation and the production tasks. Qualitative analysis indicated that the belief-bias effect was more pervasive in the production condition. In addition, the belief-bias effect was found to exist independently of the subjects' abstract reasoning ability. The results are discussed with reference to a two-stage model, in which belief is used to resolve uncertainties in inferentially produced conclusions.

Rationale

In a highly compact research format, Markovits and Nantel examined three significant aspects of the belief-bias effect in deductive reasoning. The rationale of the first aspect of their research is set forth in the following account (1989, 11, italics added):

One of the more interesting phenomena in the research on reasoning concerns the *belief-bias* effect. Several researchers have claimed that subjects tend to evaluate the logical validity of deductive arguments on the basis of their personal beliefs regarding the empirical status of the conclusion. Specifically, subjects will tend to rate an argument as valid if they think that the conclusion is empirically true, and vice versa, irrespective of the textbook validity of the argument. The reality of the belief-bias effect has been questioned (Revlin and Leirer, 1978; Revlin, Leirer, Yopp and Yopp, 1980), mainly on the grounds that some of the effects observed may be attributable to conversion effects due to subjects' idiosyncratic encoding of premises. However, Evans, Barston, and Pollard (1983) have demonstrated a strong belief-bias effect in experiments designed to control for both conversion and atmosphere effects.

The belief-bias effect has generally been found in paradigms for which subjects are presented with a specific conclusion (or a set of possible conclusions). It may be argued that, despite the most rigorous instructions, many subjects may be evaluating the empirical truth of the presented conclusion or conclusions and simply ignoring the premises, not because they cannot reason properly but because they do not properly understand the task (Henle, 1962). Such a possibility is certainly consistent with Evans et al.'s (1983) finding that subjects who accepted valid conclusions despite the influence of their beliefs referred more often to the premises than subjects who decided according to belief. One way of minimizing such a possibility and ensuring that subjects attend to the premises is to have subjects produce a conclusion. In other words, it may be argued that if the observed effects in evaluation tasks are due mainly to some process whereby subjects (mistakenly) examine only the conclusion of an argument, then forcing them to generate a conclusion from given premises should enable them to use their logical abilities more fully. Now, the effect of belief on the production of conclusions has been examined by Oakhill and Johnson-Laird (1985). They found that beliefs do tend to influence subjects' conclusion in a production task. However, they did not attempt to compare this effect with that found in an evaluation task. In addition, they compared subjects' performance with respect to believable as opposed to unbelievable conclusions, thus making the estimation of the magnitude of the effect somewhat difficult. *The main aim of the present study was therefore to replicate the effects of subjects' beliefs on the production of conclusions in a reasoning task, and to compare this effect with that found in a comparable evaluation task.*

The following rationale is provided for the second aspect of this research (Markovits & Nantel 1989, 11–12, italics added):

In the present study, we also attempted to address two further questions. First, studies in conditional reasoning have clearly shown that subjects' performance is often influenced by a variety of factors that are not directly related to the logic of the premises or the conclusion, and that it varies according to the specific logical form employed or the content of the premises. Conversion effects (Revlin et al., 1980), atmosphere bias (Woodworth and Sells, 1935), figural effects (Johnson-Laird and Steedman, 1978), and various forms of content effects (Guyotte and Sternberg, 1981; O'Brien, Costa and Overton, 1986) are all examples of such factors. Their existence makes comparisons among differing logical forms and contents somewhat hazardous. Note that Evans et al. (1983) explicitly controlled for conversion effects (as did Oakhill and Johnson-Laird, 1985), atmosphere bias, and the figural effect. While there is no evidence to suggest that their results might nonetheless have been effected by some such (as yet unknown) factor, we felt that it would be useful to replicate the basic belief-bias effect by using a method that attempted to control explicitly for both form and content effects as tightly as possible. The method chosen involved the construction of pairs of categorical syllogisms. Each syllogism involved an initial premise (major term) of the form "all A are B," which was identical for both. The second premise took one of the following forms: (1) "X is A," (2) "X is B," (3) "X is not A," and (4) "X is not B." In all cases, X was varied to produce two differing syllogisms: a neutral form that produced a conclusion for which the subject had no a priori beliefs with respect to its empirical truth; and a positive form that produced a conclusion for which the subject did have a clear belief regarding its empirical truth, and for which this belief contradicted the conclusion's logical status (i.e., if the subjects thought the conclusion was true, it was logically invalid, etc.). *By comparing the subjects' performance on the neutral and positive forms, it was felt that the belief-bias effect could be examined in a way that would eliminate any possible effects related to logical form and would minimize content variations.*

The third aspect of the Markovits and Nantel research is summarized in the following terms (1989, 12, italics added):

The final question addressed by this study concerns the possible relation between logical competence and belief-bias. Evans et al. (1983) found evidence that subjects may oscillate between competing logical and nonlogical processes. This implies that subjects do attempt to consider the logical validity of an argument by examining the premises, when they are not led to employ other criteria such as their beliefs. Without entering into the problem associated with the nature of logical competence, it appears reasonable to suppose that if subjects have difficulty in reasoning correctly from premises that are relatively content-free or abstract, they might be more prone to use nonlogical indices when these are present. *Thus there should be a relation between the ability to reason correctly during a content-free task and the performance on a task for which a belief-bias effect may exist.*

Method

The experimental materials, subjects, and procedures are described in the following section (Markovits & Nantel 1989, 12–14):

Materials

Four paper-and-pencil questionnaires were constructed. The first page of each questionnaire, which was identical for each one, presented a series of four conditional reasoning problems with abstract content. At the top of the page was written:

Suppose it is true that:
    All the XAR's are YOF's
and answer the multiple choice questions.

After this came four multiple choice questions. The first one took the following format:

(A) If a glock is a XAR, you can say
    (a) that it is certain that the glock is a YOF.
    (b) that it is certain that the glock is not a YOF.
    (c) that it is not certain whether the glock is a YOF or not.

The three other questions used the same format and presented the following statements: "(B) If a koy is a YOF, you can say"; "(C) If a glock is not a XAR, you can say"; "(D) If a koy is not a YOF, you can say." These four correspond to the logical forms *modus ponens*, *converse*, *inverse*, and *contrapositive*.

Note that in all cases, the abstract content questions proceeded the syllogisms that were to examine the belief-bias effect. It has been shown that such a procedure encourages a *logical* reasoning mode in subjects that diminishes content effects (Hawkins et al., 1984; Markovits in press). This procedure was thus designed to reduce any possible belief-bias effect and to facilitate the effect of subsequent instructions.

Two questionnaires used an evaluation paradigm. For these, the second page contained the following instructions (adapted from Evans et al., 1983):

You are going to receive a series of eight problems. You must decide whether the stated conclusion *follows logically* from the premises or not.

You must *suppose that the premises are all true* and limit yourself only to the information contained in these premises. This is very important.

At the top of the next page, the subjects received the following instructions (adapted from Evans et al., 1983):

For each problem, decide if the given conclusion *follows logically from the premises*. Circle YES if, and only if, you judge that the conclusion can be derived *unequivocally* from the given premises, otherwise circle NO.

For the *positive evaluation* questionnaire, subjects were then presented with the following eight syllogisms (four to a page):

(1) Premise 1: All things that are smoked are good for the health.
    Premise 2: Cigarettes are smoked.
    Conclusion: Cigarettes are good for the health.
(2) Premise 1: All unemployed people are poor.
    Premise 2: Rockefeller is not unemployed.
    Conclusion: Rockefeller is not poor.
(3) Premise 1: All flowers have petals.
    Premise 2: Roses have petals.
    Conclusion: Roses are flowers.
(4) Premise 1: All animals with four legs are dangerous.
    Premise 2: Poodles are not dangerous.
    Conclusion: Poodles do not have four legs.
(5) Premise 1: All mammals walk.
    Premise 2: Whales are mammals.
    Conclusion: Whales walk.
(6) Premise 1: All eastern countries are communist.
    Premise 2: Canada is not an eastern country.
    Conclusion: Canada is not communist.

(7) Premise 1:   All animals love water.
    Premise 2:   Cats do not like water.
    Conclusion: Cats are not animals.
(8) Premise 1:   All things that have a motor need oil.
    Premise 2:   Automobiles need oil
    Conclusion: Automobiles have motors.

These syllogisms include two (1, 5) of the form "all A are B, C are A, thus C are B," and two of the form "all A are B, C are not B, thus C are not A." In each of them, the conclusions were rated as unbelievable by 37 independent subjects . . . and, in each case, the conclusion was logically valid. In addition, there are two syllogisms (3, 8) of the form "all A are B, C are B, thus C are A," and two of the form "all A are B, C are not A, thus C are not B." In each of these cases, the conclusions were rated as believable and were logically invalid. In the latter two cases, it should be noted that the forms are indeterminate — that is, there is no logically valid conclusion.

The second questionnaire that used the evaluation paradigm (*neutral evaluation*) was identical to the first, but with one major difference. In all cases, the minor premise of the eight syllogisms was altered in order to make the conclusion neutral with respect to belief. . . . The resulting conclusions were:

(1) Ramadions are good for the health.
(2) Hudon is not poor.
(3) Pennes are flowers.
(4) Argomelles do not have four legs.
(5) Lapitars walk.
(6) Sylvania is not communist.
(7) Selacians are not animals.
(8) Opprobines have motors.

In addition to the two questionnaires that used an evaluation paradigm, two more that used a production paradigm were constructed. The first page of these two questionnaires, as stated above, was identical to the one described previously: it contained a set of four conditional reasoning problems with abstract content. On the second page of both production questionnaires was written the following:

You are going to receive a series of eight problems. You must *produce* a conclusion which *follows logically* from the premises.
    You must *suppose that the premises are all true* and limit yourself only to the information contained in these premises. This is very important.

At the top of the next page, the subjects received the following instructions:

For each problem, give the conclusion which *follows logically from the premises*. Formulate a conclusion only if you judge that it is possible to derive one *unequivocally* from the given premises. If you think that no conclusion can be logically and unequivocally derived from the premises, write NONE.

After this, one of the two series of eight syllogisms that were used in the evaluation questionnaires was presented (leading to two forms, *neutral production* and *positive production*), with the difference that no conclusion was presented. Space was provided for the subjects to write down a conclusion.

Procedure

The four forms of questionnaires were distributed at random among entire classes of university students. The subjects were informed that there was no time limit and that they could proceed until satisfied with their answers.

Subjects

A total of 186 French-speaking university students received one of four questionnaires. Of these, 44 received the positive production form; 48, the neutral production form; 43, the positive evaluation form; and 51, the neutral evaluation form.

Scoring

The subjects were scored both on the abstract conditional reasoning problem and on the eight syllogisms with content. For the abstract problems, the subjects' responses were rated *conditional* (for those who responded correctly to all four forms), *intermediate* (correct response to modus ponens, incorrect response to one or more of the other three forms), or *biconditional* (responding to all four forms as if the relation were "if and only if"). In addition, two response patterns were taken to indicate difficulty in accepting the given premises (Markovits, in press). Thus those subjects who gave a response of uncertainty to modus ponens, or who responded by inverting the truth value of the minor premise in the conclusion (e.g., "If P then Q, Q is true, then P is false"), were rated as having given an *uncertain* response to the abstract conditionals. In the present context, the rationale for such a scoring schema derives from the following considerations: The logically correct response to the four conditional forms is the *conditional*. Previous studies have indicated that the probability that a subject will produce the logically correct response to subsequent problems varies with the response that the subject gives on an initial problem (Markovits, 1984, in press), going from conditional, to intermediate, to biconditional, to uncertain. Thus, the scoring schema employed here explicitly uses the probability of producing the logically correct response to conditional syllogisms as an indication of reasoning ability.

Scoring on the positive evaluation syllogisms was as follows. The subjects were given one point for each time they decided that a believable response was valid or an unbelievable response was invalid. The scores thus ranged from 0 to 8. For the neutral evaluation syllogisms, the subjects were given a score of 1 for each time they gave a response equivalent to that which was scored on the positive form. Thus a subject who decided that "cigarettes are good for the health" was invalid on the positive form received 1 point while a subject who decided that "ramadions are good for the health" was invalid on the neutral form also received 1 point. The score on the neutral evaluation syllogisms thus indicates the number of times that the subjects chose the believable response for reasons related to either the logical form or the global content of the syllogisms used here, not to the believability of the conclusion.

Scoring on the positive production syllogisms was as follows — for the sake of brevity, in the following, the logical form will be referred to by the minor premise only (i.e., "A is B and C is A" will be designated by "C is A"): For the indeterminate forms ("C is B," "C is not A"), the subjects were given 1 point each time they produced a logically invalid but believable conclusion. For example, for the syllogism "all flowers have petals; roses have petals," the subjects who gave the conclusion "roses are flowers" would receive 1 point. For the other two forms ("C is A," "C is not B"), the subjects received 1 point each time they did not produce the logically valid but unbelievable conclusion. For example, for the syllogism "all things that are smoked are good for the health; cigarettes are smoked," the subjects received 1 point if they concluded that cigarettes are not good for the health," or if they did not give a firm conclusion (e.g., "cigarettes may or may not be good for the health"). For the neutral production syllogisms, the subjects were given 1 point each time they produced (or did not produce) responses equivalent to those for the positive syllogisms. These responses were identical to those in the positive form, with exception for the substituted term. For the two indeterminate syllogisms ("C is A," "C is not B"), subjects responding with, for example, "ramadions are not good for the health" or subjects not giving a firm conclusion received 1 point. Note that the scores on the production syllogisms are directly comparable to the scores on the evaluation forms, if one assumes that a subject who produces a given conclusion would evaluate that conclusion as valid and would evaluate a different conclusion as invalid. For ease of reference, these scores will be referred to as *belief* scores.

Results

The experimental findings are presented in the following account (Markovits & Nantel 1989, 14–15):

An analysis of variance using belief scores as the response variable, and type of syllogism (neutral or positive), form of presentation (evaluation or production), and performance on the abstract problems (conditional, intermediate, biconditional, or uncertain) as factors was performed. Following Conover (1980), this analysis was repeated after converting the scores on the syllogisms to rank orders. Since both analyses gave substantially the same results, only the first will be reported. This indicated significant main effects for type of syllogism . . . form of presentation . . . and performance on the abstract problem. . . . None of the interaction terms were significant. The first two main effects indicate that belief scores were higher for positive than for neutral forms, and higher for production than for

evaluation. The third main effect is due to scores generally being lower for subjects giving conditional responses to the abstract problem . . . than for those giving intermediate responses . . . which were in turn lower than for subjects giving
biconditional . . . or uncertain responses.

These results clearly support the general thesis of the existence of a belief-bias
effect in reasoning. However, the idea that the production condition should generate a lower level of belief-bias is not supported. In accord with the results
obtained by Marcus and Rips (1979), the production condition produced generally higher scores than the evaluation condition, although the effect of belief was
present for both conditions. In this context, it is interesting to take a more qualitative look at the results. Four logical forms were examined with the eight syllogisms, two of each. . . . An initial question concerns the generality of the belief-
bias effect across specific contents. The Mann-Whitney procedure was used to
examine the effect of belief-bias for single items. This indicated that for the evaluation condition, a significant effect was found for two of the eight items. For the
production condition, a significant effect was found for five of the eight items,
and a sixth item was significant at the .06 level. The two items for which no significant difference was found for the production condition were those employing
modus ponens (P is true), for which almost no belief-bias effect was obtained for
either condition. Thus, overall the belief-bias effect is generalized across the various contents employed here.

[For] the evaluation condition, the major effect of belief-bias is concentrated
on the two indeterminate forms ("C is not A," "C is B"). Mann-Whitney procedures indicate that for each of these, the scores are significantly higher for the
positive than for the neutral forms. . . . This is consistent with previous results
(Evans et al., 1983; Oakhill and Johnson-Laird, 1985). Note that while many subjects had difficulty reasoning with the "C is not B" form . . . the effect to belief
was quite small. . . . In the production condition, the effect of belief is also significant for the indeterminate forms, "C is not A" . . . and "C is B." . . . In this
case, however, there is a marginally significant difference for the "C is not B"
form.

In addition to verifying the existence of belief-bias effects, the method
employed here permits some evaluation of the extent to which belief-bias exerts
an influence on reasoning independently from any other variable. . . . [The] subjects examined here produced an overall error rate of close to 30% in reasoning
with syllogisms for which possible conclusions were neither believable nor unbelievable (neutral forms), in both the evaluation and production conditions. A
direct comparison of overall error rates indicates that the presence of belief-bias
produced an increase of 30% in the error rate in the evaluation condition, and a
corresponding increase of 63% in the production condition. This suggests that
while the presence of belief-bias does significantly influence adult reasoning,
it is clearly the case that belief-bias alone cannot account for the majority of
the errors that subjects make on items for which belief-bias may be present.
These overall results must be qualified as a function of the specific logical form

examined. If one considers the two indeterminate forms for which the effect of belief was significant for both the evaluation and production conditions, the relative increase in the error rate due to belief-bias were 49% and 80%, respectively.

In addition, these results, coupled with previous data concerning differences for individual items, suggest that belief-bias appears to be more pervasive in the production task than in the evaluation task. In the latter case, the effects of belief are more limited, both in overall scope and in the number of specific items significantly affected.

Now, in the evaluation condition, the judgment that a conclusion is invalid could imply that the subject feels that there is no valid conclusion, or that the subject feels that a conclusion other than the one presented is valid. In the production condition, subjects must produce a specific conclusion, and this condition thus permits a more specific coding of the results than does the evaluation condition. . . . [For] the two determinate forms ("C is A," "C is not B"), the effect of belief results in a higher proportion of no specific conclusion, not in any tendency to produce the overtly believable response. This is consistent with results obtained by Oakhill and Johnson-Laird (1985). For example, for the syllogism, "all eastern countries are communist; Canada is not an eastern country," subjects tend to give no firn conclusion rather than to produce the believable conclusion that "Canada is not communist." . . . [There] appears to be at least a rough relation between problem difficulty as measured by the proportion of logically correct responses on the neutral form and the effect of belief. The "C is A" form has the highest proportion of logically correct responses and the "C is B" has the lowest such proportion. These forms show, respectively, the least and greatest effect of belief.

Finally, the relation between the belief-bias effect and reasoning ability merits a more detailed examination. . . . [Belief] scores for positive content increase as reasoning performance on the abstract task decreases. However, part of this increase is attributable to the fact that less able subjects tend more often to fall into reasoning errors when belief does not play a part. Although the difference between belief scores for neutral and those for positive content does increase somewhat with decreasing performance on the abstract problem, this effect is not significant.

Commentary

The scientific work of Markovits and Nantel is an impressive demonstration of the technical specification of the interactive effects of belief-bias and logical reasoning. The effects of beliefs were demonstrated in both the production and evaluation of logical conclusions. The belief-bias effect was pervasive in the various experimental conditions. It must not be supposed that the experimental findings possess mere academic significance. A dramatic example of the vast significant effect of premise beliefs on logical conclusions can be found in Abraham Lincoln's debate with Judge Stephen Douglas concerning the Dred Scott decision that required the return of escaped slaves to their owners (as cited in Basler 1953, 231):

[W]hat follows is a short and even syllogistic argument from it [i.e., from the Dred Scott decision]. I think it follows, and submit it to the consideration of men capable of arguing, whether as I state it in syllogistic form the argument has any fault in it:

Nothing in the Constitution or laws of any State can destroy a right distinctly and expressly affirmed in the Constitution of the United States.

The right of property in a slave is distinctly and expressly affirmed in the Constitution of the United States.

Therefore, nothing in the Constitution or laws of any State can destroy the right of property in a slave.

I believe that no fault can be pointed out in that argument; assuming the truth of the premises, the conclusion, so far as I have capacity at all to understand it, follows inevitably. There is fault in it as I think, but the fault is not in the reasoning; but the falsehood in fact is a fault of the premises. I believe that the right of property in a slave *is not* distinctly and expressly affirmed in the Constitution, and Judge Douglas thinks it *is*. I believe that the Supreme Court and the advocates of that decision [the Dred Scott decision] may search in vain for the place in the Constitution where the right of property in a slave is distinctly and expressly affirmed. I say, therefore, that I think one of the premises is not true in fact.

REASONING ABOUT CAUSES AND ENABLING CONDITIONS

Philosophical inquiry has for many centuries been directed toward the explication of the nature of causation. Contemporary psychological theory and research in human causal reasoning will be considered in this section. In particular, the important research of P. W. Cheng and L. R. Novick (1991) will be described, and then a general commentary will be presented.

Probabilistic Contrast Model

In an effort to distinguish causes from enabling conditions, Cheng and Novick developed and tested the probabilistic contrast model. Central to the model are the concepts of causes as the factors that covary with effects; enabling conditions as the factors that do not vary with effects; and a focal set of events that contain the positive factors, the enabling conditions, and the effects. A computational mechanism of causality is offered (Cheng & Novick 1991, 95–96):

We propose that a single mechanism can account for the conception of causality . . . : the computation of covariation between potential causes and the effect in question over a *focal set*, a set of events implied by the context. Covariation is hypothesized to be computed over the focal set as specified by our *probabilistic contrast model* (Cheng & Novick, 1990b), which applies to discrete variables. Our model defines a *main-effect contrast* (specifying a cause involving a single factor). Δp_i, as follows:

$$\Delta p_i = p_i - p_{\bar{i}}$$

where i is a factor that describes the target event, p_i is the proportion of cases for which the effect occurs when factor i is present, and $p_{\bar{i}}$ is the proportion of cases for which the effect occurs when factor i is absent. When Δp_i is greater than some (empirically determined) criterion, then there should be a causal attribution to factor i. In other words, a cause is a factor the presence of which (relative to its absence) noticeably increases the likelihood of the effect. Only factors that are psychologically prior to the event-to-be-explained are evaluated.

As a contrast cannot be computed for a factor that is constantly present in a focal set (owing to division by zero in the computation of the proportion of the effect in the absence of the factor), the causal status of such a factor cannot be determined by events in the focal set; instead, its status is determined by events in other focal sets. In our models, such a factor is: (a) an enabling condition if it does covary with the effect in another focal set (i.e., a set of events selected under another context), but (b) causally irrelevant if it does not covary with the effect in any other focal sets.

We also defined an *interaction contrast*, which specifies a cause involving a conjunction of factors (e.g., the simultaneous presence of positively charged clouds and negatively charged clouds as the cause of thunder). By analogy to statistical contrasts, a two-way interaction contrast involving potential causal factors i and j, Δp_{ij}, is defined as follows:

$$p_{ij} = (p_{ij} - p_{\bar{i}j})(p_{i\bar{j}} - p_{\bar{i}\bar{j}})$$

where p, as before, denotes the proportion of cases in which the effect occurs when a potential contributing factor is either present or absent, as denoted by its subscripts. To our knowledge, there has not been any explicit definition of conjunctive causes in terms of contrast in previous proposals on the distinction between causes and enabling conditions.

The definitions of contrasts in equations (1) and (2) apply to inhibitory factors (i.e., factors that decrease the likelihood of an effect) as well as facilitatory factors (i.e., factors that increase the likelihood of an effect). Positive contrasts specify facilitatory causes; negative contrasts specify inhibitory causes.

We assume that a factor that does not have a noticeable probabilistic contrast will be considered causally irrelevant, independent of other constraints. That is, we assume that covariation is a necessary criterion.

The following extract illustrates the Cheng and Novick probabilistic contrast model as applied to distinguishing among causes, enabling conditions, and irrelevant causes in the case of a focal set of lightning and forest fire events (Cheng & Novick 1991, 97, italics added):

Now, assume that lightning struck the forest at the place where the fire started immediately before it started. Applying our model to the focal set of events, we see that the proportion of cases for which fire occurs in the presence of lightning is greater than the proportion of cases for which fire occurs in the absence of lightning (i.e., lightning covaries with fire). Lightning is therefore a cause. In contrast, the corresponding difference in proportions cannot be computed for oxygen, because oxygen is present in every event in that set. Oxygen does covary with fire in other focal sets, however; it is therefore an enabling condition. Finally, the presence of stones in the forest, which does not covary with forest fire in any focal set, would be considered causally irrelevant. *Thus, covariation computed over a focal set of events can differentiate among causes, enabling conditions, and causally irrelevant factors for an abnormal event such as a forest fire.*

In the following paragraphs, Cheng and Novick relate their probabilistic contrast model of causality to the logic of necessary and sufficient causes and argue for the predictive usefulness of this model (1991, 97–98, italics added):

Cheng and Novick (1990a, 1990b) drew a distinction between the data on which the causal inference process operates and the process of inference computation itself. In the present context, one can entirely explain the paradoxical distinction between causes and enabling conditions by a shift in the set of data on which the distinction is based from the set of data on which the logical identity of causes and enabling conditions is based. *Although causes and enabling conditions hold the same relationship to the target effect in terms of necessity and sufficiency with respect to the universal set of events in one's knowledge base, they do not do so with respect to the focal set. The distinction between causes and enabling conditions therefore does not contradict the status of these factors in terms of necessity and sufficiency within the focal set.*

The computation of covariation over a focal set of events, rather than over the universal set of events that are causally relevant to fires (for example), maximizes the predictive value of the causes so identified for the focal set. If a primary goal of causal explanation is prediction, then the computation of covariation over a focal set is clearly adaptive. Consider some candidate answers to the question on the cause of the forest fire mentioned above in the context of the goal of predicting the next forest fire. The answer "the presence of oxygen" (which would covary with fire if all events in one's knowledge base that are causally relevant to fires are considered) is clearly not predictive of when the next fire will occur in the forest, for the obvious reason that oxygen is always present for all events in the forest (the focal set with which the questioner is concerned). In contrast, the answers "the lightning" or "the unusual dryness of the weather", which are based on the computation over a pragmatically restricted subset of events, are much more predictive of the next fire in the forest. *The computation of covariation over a focal set therefore identifies causal factors that are more useful among those that are equally true.*

Focal Sets and the Computation of Covariation

The probabilistic contrast model provides for the influence of differing contexts on the differentiation of causes and enabling conditions by the computation of covariation of events in a particular focal set. Figure 2.1 contains examples of the computational procedure (Cheng & Novick 1991, 98–100, italics added):

The figure is assumed to represent the entire set of events that are relevant to a particular effect in a hypothetical person's knowledge base. In the figure, each letter (e.g., q) represents a potential causal factor. A bar above a letter (e.g., q̄) denotes the absence of that factor. An event is represented by a sequence of letters (e.g., q̄rs) denoting the conjunct of those factors in the event. The presence of the effect for an event is represented by placing the event in larger bold type. The absence of the effect for an event is represented by regular (small and non-bold) letters. Finally, loops enclosing events denote subsets of events selected under various contexts. That is, each enclosed subset represents a different focal set.

As can be seen in the figure, with respect to the universal set of events, factors q and r are individually necessary (i.e., $p_{\bar{q}} = p_{\bar{r}} = 0$) and jointly sufficient (i.e., $p_q < 1$, $p_r < 1$, but $p_{qr} = 1$) for the occurrence of the effect. Now consider subsets A and B. For each of these subsets, one factor covaries with the effect. For example, in set A, because $p_r = 1$, and $p_{\bar{r}} = 0$, r should be perceived as a cause of the effect for that subset. (Factor r is sufficient and necessary for the effect within set A. For simplicity of exposition, only deterministic covariations are illustrated in the figure, but the model applies in the same manner to probabilistic covariations.) Factor q, however, remains constantly present in that focal set. A contrast for q therefore cannot be computed (within that set, q is insufficient for the effect and its necessity is undermined). Factor q therefore should not be selected as a

FIGURE 2.1
Computation of Covariation

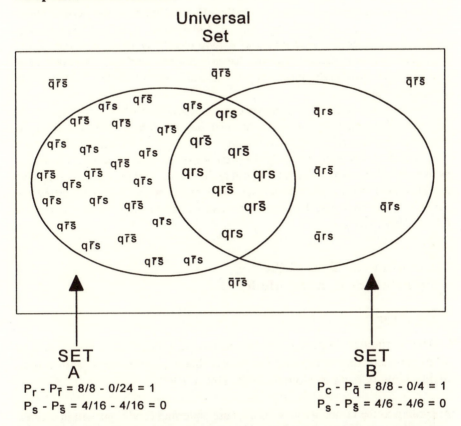

Universal
Set

SET
A
$P_r - P_{\bar{r}} = 8/8 - 0/24 = 1$
$P_s - P_{\bar{s}} = 4/16 - 4/16 = 0$

SET
B
$P_c - P_{\bar{q}} = 8/8 - 0/4 = 1$
$P_s - P_{\bar{s}} = 4/6 - 4/6 = 0$

Note: This figure depicts computation of covariation within focal sets according to the probabilistic contrast model as an explanation of the distinction among causes, enabling conditions, and causally irrelevant factors. Each letter represents a factor. A bar above a letter denotes the absence of that factor. An event is represented by a sequence of letters denoting the conjunct of those factors in the event. The presence of the effect for an event is represented by placing the event in larger type. The absence of the effect for an event is represented by regular letters. Finally, loops enclosing the events denote focal sets.

Source: P. W. Cheng and L. R. Novick, "Causes versus Enabling Conditions," *Cognition* 40 (1991): 83–120. Reprinted with permission of Elsevier Science Publishers.

cause. But it is an enabling condition because it does covary with the effect in another focal set, set B. (It would have been causally irrelevant if it did not covary with the effect in any focal set.) Conversely, in set B, *q* covaries with the effect, as mentioned, whereas *r* remains constant. Only *q*, therefore, should be perceived as the cause of the effect for that subset. *Varying the relevant focal set thus alters which factor should be considered a cause and which an enabling condition.*

Notice that although s is sometimes present and sometimes absent in each subset, its presence or absence does not covary with the effect in either subset. Factor s is therefore causally irrelevant to the effect (at least for the person whose knowledge is represented in the figure). *Covariation over specified subsets therefore accounts for the distinctions among causes, enabling conditions, and causally irrelevant factors.* Recall that by comparison, the normality view requires a separate preliminary stage to discriminate conditions from causally irrelevant factors.

We have proposed that covariation computed over a focal set serves as the criterion for distinguishing among causes, enabling conditions, and causally irrelevant factors, regardless of the normality of the event to be explained. [Figure 2.1] illustrates this point. In set A, the presence of the effect is abnormal, whereas in set B it is normal. Contrasts regarding the presence of the effect for each set are illustrated in the figure. Contrasts can likewise be calculated regarding the absence of the effect, which of course have the complementary status with respect to normality in each set.

Experimental Tests of the Probabilistic Contrast Model

Overview

The distinction between causes and enabling conditions was tested in an experiment that compared the probabilistic contrast view with a normality view (Cheng & Novick 1991, 109–110):

According to the normality view, causes are abnormal conditions within a given context, whereas enabling conditions are normal conditions within the context. In contrast, according to the probabilistic contrast model, causes are factors that covary with the effect within a relevant set of events (regardless of the normality of the factors); and enabling conditions are factors that remain constant within the focal set (hence their covariation with the effect cannot be computed for that set), but are known to covary with the effect in some other subset of events (i.e., are causally relevant). Normality per se, according to this view, should have no effect on the perception of causes versus enabling conditions. We report an experiment that tested these two views.

We tested our probabilistic contrast model by manipulating the focal set on which subjects were expected to compute their causal inferences. The focal sets were presented in the form of two scenarios, which differed in the factor that covaried with the effect and the factors that remained constant. In addition to manipulating the focal set, we manipulated normality, in both its statistical and idealistic senses. For each scenario, the covarying factor is prevalent (hence a default in one version but rare (hence not a default) in another). Furthermore, whereas one of the scenarios described a covarying factor that was desired (i.e., an ideal), the other scenario described a covarying factor that was not desired (i.e., a deviation from an ideal).

Both scenarios concerned plant growth. One was about the growth of a weed, dandelions, in a family yard (an undesired outcome) and the other was about the maturation of corn plants in corn fields (a desired outcome). In each scenario, one factor covaried with the effect. This factor differed across the scenarios (sunlight in the dandelion scenario vs. nutrients in the soil in the corn scenario). The remaining factors were held constant in each scenario: two of these factors were necessary for the effect according to subjects' prior knowledge (water in both scenarios in addition to one of the above two factors) and one of them was not (the presence of a house next to the plants). At the end of each scenario was a causal question about plant growth. Subjects were asked to indicate the causal status (cause, mere condition, causally irrelevant, and inhibitor) of each of the four factors.

Statistical normality was operationalized in the scenarios by specifying the positive value of the covarying factor as occurring in either most or few cases in the given context. For example, in the prevalent version of the ideal scenario, four out of the five corn fields tended by a farmer had virgin soil (the positive value of the covarying factor) whereas the fifth had its soil depleted of nutrients by previous farming. To ensure that virgin soil was perceived as a default in the given context, the farmer was described in the scenario as a pioneer settling in a valley where few people had reached and farmed. In contrast, in the rare version of the scenario, many corn plants matured in only one of the five corn fields. This field had virgin soil whereas the other four fields had depleted soil. To ensure that virgin soil was not perceived as a default, the farm was described in the scenario as inherited through many generations of farmers in a poor country. Because our operational definition of statistical normality satisfies the more stringent interpretation of being a majority, it also satisfies the less stringent one of being a default (Kahneman and Miller, 1986).

Before subjects read the scenarios, they were given the brief explanation of the distinction between causes and mere conditions. . . . As mentioned earlier, because the example in the explanation fits the variants of the normality view as well as the probabilistic-contrast view, any results differentiating the two views must be due to subjects' intuitive understanding of the distinction.

To measure the perceived focal sets, subjects were asked to rate how accurately each of three expanded questions that specified different focal sets reflected their interpretation of the causal question in each scenario. To measure the perceived "default" values, subjects were asked to indicate the value of the covarying factor (e.g., rich soil vs. soil depleted of nutrients) that they expected in general in each scenario.

The following paragraphs provide an account of and the rationale for systematic experimental predictions (Cheng & Novick 1991, 110):

The probabilistic-contrast view predicts that the two scenarios, which differ in the factor that yields a large probabilistic contrast (sunlight in the dandelion scenario vs. nutrients in the corn scenario) and the factors that are constantly present in the scenario (all variables besides the one with the large contrast), will produce different causes and enabling conditions. Moreover, it predicts that the normality of the covarying factor in the focal set (whether it is prevalent or rare and whether it fits the ideal or deviates from it) will not influence judgments on the causal status of any factor. In particular, it predicts that a factor that covaries with the effect in the focal set, even a statistically or idealistically normal one, will be considered a cause and be distinguished from conditions that are constantly present in the focal set.

In contrast, the statistical normality view predicts that within each scenario (dandelion or corn), only in the rare (non-default) versions should conditions be considered causes; in the prevalent (default) versions, they should be considered enabling conditions, despite large probabilistic contrasts for these factors within the focal set. The idealistic normality view, however, predicts that only conditions that deviate from an ideal (i.e., those in the dandelion scenario but not those in the corn scenario) should be considered causes.

Method

Experimental subjects, procedure, materials, and design are presented in the following (Cheng & Novick 1991, 111–113):

Subjects and procedure

The subjects were 78 UCLA students, who participated in partial fulfillment of requirements for their introductory psychology class. Each subject received a 6-page booklet as a distractor task in a memory experiment conducted on individual subjects. The subjects completed the task in 7–10 minutes.

Materials and design

The first page of the booklet was the explanation of causes versus enabling conditions [distinction]. The last page of the booklet was the prior knowledge. The rest of the materials pertained to two brief scenarios, at the end of each of which was a question about an event in the scenario.

Subjects received the prevalent version of one scenario and the rare version of the other scenario, with the order of statistical normality and scenarios (i.e., idealistic normality) counterbalanced across subjects. Subjects were randomly assigned to one of the four combinations of the ordering of statistical normality and scenario by an experimenter who had no knowledge of the conditions. There were no order effects in the data; the order manipulations will therefore not be considered further.

Following is the prevalent version of the ideal scenario, in which amount of nutrients covaried with plant growth and the amounts of sunlight and water were constant within the focal set:

A young pioneer Greg built a cabin in a valley. He recently cleared an area next to his cabin, and planted corn in five fields. Although few other farmers had been in this valley, one of Greg's fields had had most of the nutrients in the soil depleted by several years of planting by a previous farmer. The other four fields were the ones that Greg had just cleared and had never been farmed before. At harvest time, Greg found that there were a lot of mature corn plants in the four new fields. But none of the corn plants in the old field matured. The plants in all five fields received the same amounts of water and sunlight since they were right next to each other. *What caused the corn plants to grow in the four recently cleared fields?*

The rare version of this scenario was identical to the above, with the exception that Greg, instead of being a pioneer settling in a valley with mostly virgin soil, "lives in a valley in a poor country, on a farm inherited through many generations in his family." Furthermore, the ratio of rich-to-depleted soil was reversed: four of Greg's fields had had most of the nutrients in the soil depleted by many years of planting by his predecessors, and the fifth was one that he had just cleared.

Following is the rare version of the non-ideal scenario, in which sunlight covaried with plant growth and the amounts of fertilizer and water were constant within the implied focal set:

A little boy Brad lives with his family in a wooded area. He noticed that there were dandelions covering the small open areas of his family's yard, but that there were no dandelions under the shade of the two large oak trees. He knows that sprinklers are distributed evenly over the yard. One day during a rainstorm he put jars out all over the yard and discovered that the amount of rain reaching the ground was roughly the same under the oak trees and in the open areas of the yard. He also found out that the soil was the same in all parts of the yard and that all parts of the yard had received the same amount of fertilizer. *What causes the dandelions to grow in the small open areas of the yard?*

The prevalent version of this scenario was identical to the above, with the exception that Brad, instead of living in a wooded area, lived in a barren area with few trees. In addition, the open areas of his yard were described as "large" and the oak trees were described as "small".

Questions and predictions

Subjects were asked four questions about the scenarios they received. The first question asked subjects to indicate whether each of four factors was a "cause (not a mere condition)", a "mere condition (not a cause)", or "irrelevant (neither a cause nor a mere condition)" for the growth of the respective plants (corn and dandelions). For the corn scenario, these factors were water, the farmer's house, sunlight, and nutrients in the soil. For the dandelion scenario, these factors were water, fertilizer, sunlight, and the boy's house. The probabilistic contrast model predicts that subjects will be more likely to pick a particular factor as a cause in the scenario in which it covaries with the effect in the implied focal set than in the scenario in which it remains constant. Neither statistical nor idealistic normality should affect subjects' responses. Necessary factors that remain constant should be mere conditions, and unnecessary factors should be causally irrelevant.

The second question asked whether each of four factors "inhibited" the growth of the respective plants in the given context. For the corn scenario, these factors were lack of water, the farmer's house, sunlight, and lack of nutrients in the soil. For the dandelion scenario, these factors were water, lack of fertilizer, lack of sunlight, and the boy's house. (Notice that two of the three necessary factors in each scenario were made negative by changing from the presence of the factor in the first question to the absence of the factor in the second question.) This question was included as a further test of the idealistic normality view. Asking about inhibition rather than facilitation reverses the desirability of the conditions. Whereas the presence of nutrients in the corn scenario (leading to the maturation of the plants) was desired, the absence of nutrients in one or more of the fields (leading to the failure of the plants to mature) was not. The idealistic normality view therefore predicts that whereas the desired presence of each necessary factor (e.g., nutrients in the corn scenario) would be an enabling condition, the undesired absence of the same factor in the identical scenario would be an inhibitory cause. Conversely, this view predicts that whereas the undesired presence of each necessary factor (e.g., sunlight in the dandelion scenario) would be a cause, the desired absence of the same factor in that scenario would not be an inhibitory cause. In contrast, the probabilistic-contrast view predicts that the factor that covaries with the effect in the focal set would be judged to be a cause, and the absence of that factor would be judged to be inhibitory, regardless of whether the presence or absence of that factor is desirable within the context.

The third question measured subjects' focal sets. It asked subjects to rate on a 7-point scale three expanded versions of the causal question in terms of how accurately each reflected their interpretation of the causal question (7 = very accurately, 1 = very inaccurately). Each expansion focussed the causal question on a comparison along a different one of the three relevant dimensions mentioned in the scenario. For example, one of the expansions for the causal question in the sunlight scenario was: "What caused the dandelions to grow where there was ample fertilizer, compared to other places where there was not ample fertilizer (assuming that all places had roughly the same amounts of water and sunlight)?"

The fourth and final question asked subjects to indicate the value of the covarying factor that they expected in general in each scenario. In the corn scenario, the question was, "Do most places in the valley where Greg lived (including his fields) have rich soil or soil depleted of nutrients?" In the dandelion scenario, the question was, "Do most places in the area where Brad lives (including his yard) receive direct sunlight, or are most places in the shade?" This question was to ensure that our manipulation of prevalence was effective and that the prevalent covarying factors did fit the definition of normality in terms of being a default.

Results and Discussion

Table 2.1 presents the data bearing on the experimental predictions. Experimental findings are summarized and discussed in the following account (Cheng & Novick 1991, 114–116, italics added):

TABLE 2.1
Percentage of Subjects Indicating a Factor To Be a Cause or a Mere Condition in Experiment 2 for Prevalent and Rare Causes in an Ideal and a Non-ideal Context

	Statistical Normality	
	Prevalent	**Rare**
Context in which "nutrients" has a large contrast and other factors are constant (corn scenario — ideal)		
N	32	35
Sunlight		
Cause	12	11
Mere Condition	∝	—
Nutrients		
Cause	**91**	**89**
Mere Condition	9	11
Water		
Cause	12	11
Mere Condition	**88**	**77**
House		
Cause	0	0
Mere Condition	3	6
Context in which "sunlight" has a large contrast and other factors are constant (dandelion scenario — non-ideal)		
N	37	32
Sunlight		
Cause	**95**	**91**
Mere Condition	5	9
Nutrients		
Cause	11	3
Mere Condition	**81**	**84**

TABLE 2.1 (cont.)

	Statistical Normality	
	Prevalent	**Rare**
Water		
Cause	8	3
Mere Condition	**84**	**88**
House		
Cause	0	0
Mere Condition	5	0

Note: Subjects whose ratings in the focal-set question reveal that they did not adopt the focal sets assumed by this analysis are excluded from this table. Numbers in **bold** type indicate the percentages of subjects who chose the responses predicted by the probabilistic contrast model.

Source: P. W. Cheng and L. R. Novick, "Causes versus Enabling Conditions," *Cognition* 40 (1991): 83–120. Reprinted with permission of Elsevier Science Publishers.

We turn now to the critical question on causes versus mere conditions. The probabilistic contrast model predicts that subjects should be more likely to choose a particular factor as a cause in the scenario in which it covaried with the effect in the implied focal set than in the scenario in which it was constant, regardless of the prevalence of the desirability of the factor. The results were as predicted by this model [see Table 2.1]. Because the model specifies its predictions with respect to the focal set, our analyses below are restricted to subjects for whom our focal set manipulation was effective. An average of 90% of the subjects indicated nutrients to be a cause for the corn scenario, compared to only 7% who did so for the dandelion scenario, $\chi^2(1, N = 69) = 43.8$, p < .001 for the prevalent version of each of the two scenarios, and $\chi^2(1, N = 67) = 48.9$, p < .001 for the rare versions. Conversely, an average of 93% of the subjects indicated sunlight to be a cause for the dandelion scenario, compared to only 12% who did so for the corn scenario, $\chi^2(1, N = 69) = 47.1$, p < .001 for the prevalent version of each of the two scenarios, and $\chi^2(1, N = 67) = 42.0$, p < .001 for the rare versions. The third necessary factor, the presence of water, was constant in both scenarios. As predicted, it was indicated as a mere condition by most subjects (84%) in both scenarios. The fourth factor, the presence of the protagonist's house, was rarely indicated as a cause or a mere condition. They were indicated as irrelevant by most subjects in both the corn and the dandelion scenarios (96% and 97%, respectively).

As should be evident from a comparison of the results across the prevalent and rare versions of each scenario in [Table 2.1], the prevalence of a factor had no discernible effect on causal judgments for any of the four factors. The comparison was not statistically significant for any of the factors. Our results clearly show that subjects discriminated between prevalent factors that covary within the focal set (these were identified as causes) and prevalent conditions that were constant (these were identified as enabling conditions).

Recall that the idealistic normality view predicts that only conditions that deviate from the ideal should be selected as causes; that is, the presence of sunlight in the dandelion scenario should be the only cause, and the absence of nutrients in the corn scenario should be the only inhibitor. Contradicting these predictions but in support of the probabilistic contrast view, the positive values of both contextually covarying factors — the presence of nutrients in the corn scenario (a desired state) and the presence of sunlight in the dandelion scenario (an undesired state) — were judged to be causes (90% and 93%, respectively). Similarly, the negative values of both covarying factors — the absence of nutrients in the corn scenario (an undesired state) and the absence of sunlight in the dandelion scenario (a preferred state) — were judged to be inhibitors (94% and 96%, respectively). (Also as predicted by probabilistic contrasts, no other factor was considered an inhibitor in either scenario; less than 2% of the responses indicated other factors to be inhibitors.)

These results clearly show that factors that covaried with the effect in the set of events implied by the context, regardless of their prevalence or desirability, were perceived as causes (so identified by 92% of the subjects on average). In contrast, factors that remained constant in that focal set, but were nonetheless known to be necessary for the occurrence of the effect, were relegated to the status of mere conditions (so identified by 83% of the subjects on average).

Conclusion

The following presents the concluding analysis of the Cheng and Novick experimental research (1991, 116–117):

The results of our experiments support our probabilistic contrast model over a number of alternative explanations of the distinction between causes and enabling conditions. Let us briefly summarize the basis for this conclusion.

The normality, conversational, and probabilistic contrast views localize the explanation for the distinction between causes and enabling conditions at different stages. Both variants of the normality view explain the distinction at the inference stage. They hypothesize that people perceive a distinction between causes and enabling conditions despite their identity in terms of necessity and sufficiency because natural causal induction uses a rule that is not formulated in those terms. . . . Finally, the probabilistic contrast view traces the distinction to a stage before the process of inference begins. It explains the distinction by differences in the patterns of data that correspond to causes and enabling conditions for a focal set. Although causes and enabling conditions hold the same relationship with the target effect in terms of necessity and sufficiency with respect to the universal set of events in one's knowledge base, they do not do so with respect to the focal set. The probabilistic contrast view therefore resolves the puzzling deviation from characterization in terms of necessity and sufficiency by denying the existence of such a deviation.

Our results clearly support the probabilistic-contrast view. In [the experiment], we demonstrated the effect of patterns of data in the focal set on the distinction between the causes and enabling conditions. We manipulated the patterns of data in the focal set and confirmed the effectiveness of our manipulation by measuring subjects' identification of the contextually implied focal sets. Our results show that factors that covaried with the effect in the focal set were perceived as causes, and necessary factors that were kept constant in the focal set were perceived as enabling conditions.

Our results also provide evidence against the variants of the normality view. [The experiment] clearly shows that factors that covaried with the effect in the set of events implied by the context were perceived as causes, regardless of their prevalence or their status as a default or an ideal. By identifying the focal set, we have shown that the same inferential rules underlie the concept of causality in everyday life, where causes are typically statistically abnormal or deviate from an ideal, and in scientific situations, where causes are often statistically normal and do not deviate from an ideal.

Commentary

Theories of causality have advanced from anomistic superstition, to rational analysis, to mathematical functions. This development is most marked in the physical sciences, where the human concept of causation has been replaced by abstract mathematical symbols and equations. Philosophical accounts of causation — from Aristotle's typology of formal, final, material, and efficient causes to Mackie's theory of causal fields — are largely verbal constructions tied to everyday psychological experience. The mathematization of this commonsense psychology would mark an advancement in the development of a scientific psychology. The computational mechanisms that distinguish causes from enabling conditions are the most sophisticated components of Cheng and Novick's probabilistic-contrast model as it replaces verbal analysis with mathematical equations. The experimental research of Cheng and Novick supports their computational model, and replication and extension are warranted; however, in practical human affairs, as in legal reasoning, causation is psychologically mercurial and offers formidable challenges to its mathematization.

3

Analogical Thinking

THE ANALOGICAL RETRIEVAL BY CONSTRAINT SATISFACTION SYSTEM

Analogies are present in many varieties of thinking. Poetic analogies stir the imagination and scientific analogies clarify problems. What are the principles governing effective analogical thinking? What conditions control the retrieval of appropriate analogies from human memory? The latter question was investigated by P. Thagard, K. J. Holyoak, G. Nelson, and D. Gochfeld. Their interesting research into analog retrieval by constraint satisfaction (ARCS) will be described, and then a commentary will be offered.

Analogical Retrieval and Constraint Satisfaction

Overview

The following account summarizes the research of Thagard, Holyoak, Nelson, and Gochfeld (1990, 259):

We describe a computational model of how analogs are retrieved from memory using simultaneous satisfaction of a set of semantic, structural, and pragmatic constraints. The model is based on psychological evidence suggesting that human memory retrieval tends to favor analogs that have several kinds of correspondences with the structure that prompts retrieval: semantic similarity, isomorphism, and pragmatic relevance. We describe ARCS, a program that demonstrates how these constraints can be used to select relevant analogs by forming a network of hypotheses and attempting to satisfy the constraints simultaneously. ARCS has been tested on several data bases that display both its psychological plausibility and computational power.

General Theory

The Thagard, Holyoak, Nelson, and Gochfeld theory of analogical retrieval is set forth in the following section. This theory assumes that appropriate analogical retrieval is governed by the coordinated effect of semantic, isomorphic, and pragmatic constraints (1990, 260–268):

A theory of analog retrieval should be broad enough to cover the rich diversity of kinds of analogical thinking. In cognitive science, most attention has been paid to analogical problem solving, in which a stored *source* analog is used to suggest a solution to a posed *target* problem. Most psychological experiments have concerned *cross-domain* analogical problem solving, in which the source and target derive from different domains (e.g., [Gentner & Gentner, 1983; Gick & Holyoak, 1980, 1983; Holyoak & Koh, 1987]). In contrast, much AI research has been restricted to the use of analogies within a single domain, often under the heading of *case-based* problem solving and planning [Hammond, 1986; Kolodner & Simpson, 1988].

But problem solving is not the only purpose of analogy. For example, analogies are often used in explanations, when we use a source analog to provide understanding of a target phenomenon [Thagard, Cohen, & Holyoak, 1989]. Sometimes the source generates understanding without much modification, but in other cases the source is used to form new explanatory hypotheses, a process that Thagard [1988] calls *analogical abduction*. Analogies can be used, not only to form hypotheses, but to help evaluate them [Thagard, 1989]. Analogies are often used in political, historical, and legal arguments, functioning to convince someone that a particular conclusion is warranted. . . . Finally, literary analogies can have an evocative function, calling forth relevant emotional responses to past events or situations with established emotional content.

In common with many theorists, we decompose analogy into:

(1) retrieval or selection of a plausibly useful analog,
(2) mapping between source and the target,
(3) transfer of information in the source for appropriate use with the target,
(4) subsequent learning.

Sometimes an analog is directly given, as when a student is told to think of a chemical bond as a kind of tug-of-war [Thagard, Cohen, & Holyoak, 1988]. In such cases, the use of analogy primarily requires *mapping* one analog onto the other. Our direct concern in this paper is only with (1), retrieval of an analog in the absence of any external guidance as to what information in memory is relevant. We have previously proposed ACME, a constraint-satisfaction model of analogy mapping [Holyoak & Thagard, 1989]. Because there is evidence that the constraints on analogical access overlap in important ways with the constraints on analogical mapping, the ARCS model of retrieval proposed in the present paper shares many features with the ACME model of mapping, as will be discussed below. The output of the ARCS retrieval process can in fact serve as input to ACME simulations.

Computationally, retrieval of analogs is a difficult problem. A computational system must have at least the following capabilities:

(1) It must efficiently find relevant analogs. In a small data base, this can be trivial, since exhaustive search can be applied. But in a large data base, exhaustive search will be too slow.

(2) The system must be able to screen out analogs that are less relevant, so that it does not get swamped by retrieving unusable numbers of cases. Some sort of comparative mechanism must ensure that the most relevant analogs are selected over others.

(3) If the system is intended to be a psychological model, the analogs it retrieves and the processes by which it does so should correspond to human performance as exhibited in controlled psychological experiments. Our project is to model human cognition, but we acknowledge the possibility of AI models aimed more at engineering adequacy than cognitive modeling. At least in the present state of AI, cognitive and engineering aims seem slightly convergent, as a system that successfully emulated human analog retrieval would clearly surpass the performance of current AI models of analogy.

To put it simply, the problem of analog retrieval is how to get what you want from memory without getting more than you can use. Indeed, this is the core problem of memory retrieval in general. . . . In particular, the model assumes an organized store of concepts to which representations of particular episodes are linked. Representations of episodes are viewed as decomposable into more elementary elements, which provide multiple potential retrieval cues. The memory system is content addressable, in that any element of a stored representation can potentially serve as a basis for access to the entire representation. Retrieval is an essentially parallel process that involves comparison of the target analog to representations of potential source analogs in memory.

As we will see, however, our model of analog retrieval goes beyond current theories of general memory retrieval in its sensitivity to configural information concerning the relational structure of the analogs. The distinctive characteristic of the retrieval of analogs, as opposed to simple associative retrieval, is that the basis for retrieval is not simply shared elements, but also comparable *patterns* of elements. . . . The present model provides a mechanism for integrating Gestalt-like sensitivity to relational patterns into an associative memory.

Whereas the process of analog retrieval is viewed as involving parallel comparisons to multiple representations in memory, mapping and transfer are apparently more restricted, in that people generally use one analog at a time when engaged in the mapping and transfer stages of problem solving, explanation, and argument. It is therefore important that the retrieval process be designed so as to tend to select only the most promising potential analogs as candidates for more detailed subsequent analyses.

A Constraint-Satisfaction Theory

In our paper on mapping [Holyoak & Thagard, 1989], we identified three major kinds of constraints that have been proposed to govern how parts of two analogs can be placed in correspondence with each other: semantic similarity, isomorphism, and pragmatic centrality. These constraints were treated not as absolute requirements on successful mappings, but rather as *pressures* that operate to some *degree* [Hofstadter, 1984]. We argued that all three types of constraints are involved in analogical mapping. Here we will briefly review the distinctions among these three classes of constraints and the psychological evidence regarding their impact on the retrieval of analogs.

Semantic similarity

Two analogs are semantically similar to the extent that the predicates used in the representations of the two analogs are semantically similar. We use the term "semantics" here in the lexical sense [Cruse, 1986], not in the formal, model-theoretic sense. Two predicates are semantically similar if they are identical or if they participate in lexical relations such as synonymy, hyponymy (representing things of the same kind) and meronymy (representing things similar with respect to part-whole relations).

Numerous psychological experiments indicate that retrieval of analogs by humans is very sensitive to the degree of semantic overlap between the target analog that provides retrieval cues and the source analog to be found in memory [Gentner & Landers, 1985; Gick & Holyoak, 1980, 1983; Gilovich, 1981; Holyoak & Koh, 1987; Rattermann & Gentner, 1987; Ross, 1984, 1987, 1989]. Such overlap depends on the semantic similarity of the concepts used to represent the analogs. For example, Holyoak and Koh [1987] found that subjects given a problem of finding a way to use an X-ray to destroy a tumor were much more likely to retrieve an analogous problem concerning using a laser to fuse a filament in a lightbulb than they were to retrieve an analogous problem concerning using ultrasound to fuse a filament. This difference appeared to reflect the fact that X-ray devices are more like lasers than like ultrasound devices. Other similar studies using analogs that lacked *any* apparent similar elements (e.g., a source analog involving use of an army to capture a fortress) have found that people are often unable to retrieve dissimilar analogs, even though such analogs could readily be used to aid in problem solving once the person was reminded of their relevance by the experimenter [Catrambone & Holyoak, 1990; Gick & Holyoak, 1980, 1983; Spencer & Weisberg, 1986].

We view the role of semantic similarity in analog retrieval as simply a special case of its dominant role in general memory retrieval processes in humans. Because semantic links typically provide fundamental retrieval pathways, we would expect that positive similarity between at least one pair of elements in a target and source analog will be a necessary (but not sufficient) precondition for retrieval. We know of no cases of human analog retrieval in which the analogs had no semantic similarity. In contrast there are special cases of mapping between pairs of analogs that depend only on isomorphism, for example mapping abstract relations of number addition with abstract relations of set union [Holyoak & Thagard, 1989]. The problem of mapping two given analogs is different from the problem of selecting an analog for a single given target from a large memory that contains numerous potential analogs. Our model treats semantic similarity as the dominant constraint on retrieval, but not the only one.

Isomorphism

The overwhelming evidence that semantic similarity plays a major role in analog retrieval has contributed to the relative neglect of configural effects on reminding. We contend that an analog is more likely to be retrieved the greater the degree of isomorphism it has with the structure that initiates the retrieval. Informally, isomorphism is a matter of having the same configuration. A more exact notion can be developed by assuming that structures can be represented by propositions consisting of predicates and arguments. Then two structures are isomorphic if there is a one-to-one correspondence between them that preserves structural consistency, where structural consistency requires that if two propositions are mapped, then their constituent predicates and arguments should also map [Falkenhainer, Forbus, & Gentner, 1986, 1989/90; Gentner, 1983]. . . . Isomorphism is conceptually distinct from semantic similarity, in that two structures can be perfectly isomorphic even though they share no identical or similar elements [Holyoak & Thagard, 1989; Palmer, 1989]. Two structures can fail to be isomorphic because the best correspondence between them is not one-to-one or does not preserve relational structure. Mathematically, isomorphism is an all-or-none matter, but we speak of degree of isomorphism informally as the extent to which the best correspondence between them is not one-to-one and structurally consistent. Like Falkenhainer et al. [1989/90], our notion of structural consistency includes higher-order relations such as "cause" that can take propositions as arguments. For example, if a proposition $cause(p,q)$ stating that p causes q is to be placed in correspondence with $cause(r,s)$, then the predicates and arguments of p and q should correspond, respectively, to the predicates and arguments of r and s.

There is some evidence from studies of analogy that retrieval is indeed sensitive to isomorphism. Experiments reported by Gentner [Gentner, 1989; Gentner

& Gentner, 1983] primarily showed the effects of semantic similarity on retrieval, but they found that higher-order relational commonalities also promote access. Holyoak and Koh [1987] found evidence that *both* structural consistency and semantic similarity affect the probability that a source analog will be spontaneously retrieved and used. The materials they used were various versions of the lightbulb and tumor analogs discussed earlier. One variation in the source lightbulb stories involved the reason a single large force could not be used to fuse the filament: either because the force would break the delicate glass surrounding the filament, or because no single large force was available. In both versions the successful solution was to use multiple converging weak forces. The former "similar constraint" version was more structurally consistent with the tumor problem, in which a single strong laser could not be used because it would damage healthy tissue surrounding the tumor. Holyoak and Koh found that subjects were more likely to spontaneously apply the similar-constraint version of the source analog. (The term "constraint" here refers to the specific constraint on the problem solution in the experimental materials, and should not be confused with the general analogy constraint of isomorphism.)

Ross [1989] performed a series of experiments in which subjects had to apply probability principles that were initially illustrated by a single concrete word problem. Subjects were then asked to solve transfer word problems. Ross varied whether the overall cover stories of the source and target problems were highly similar (e.g., two problems involving the IBM motor pool) or dissimilar (e.g., a motor-pool problem and a nursery-school problem). This manipulation of semantic similarity of the analogs was crossed with a variation in degree of structural consistency. In the consistent conditions, similar types of entities mapped onto corresponding variables in the relevant equations (e.g., people mapped to people, artifacts to artifacts), whereas in the inconsistent conditions the required mappings were crossed (people to artifacts and artifacts to people). Ross found that inconsistent mappings impaired access to the source, but only when the overall cover story was similar. Thus relatively high semantic similarity was a necessary condition for obtaining an effect of structural consistency. As we will see, this type of interaction between semantic and structural constraints on retrieval is predicted by the ARCS model.

Pragmatic centrality

As we suggested . . . , analogies have various purposes. The purpose of an analogy in problem solving is to help accomplish the goals of the problem. Clearly, a retrieval system attuned to increase the retrieval of analogs relevant to goal accomplishment would contribute more to problem-solving effectiveness than a retrieval system that lacked sensitivity to goals. We therefore postulate that one of the constraints on analog retrieval is pragmatic centrality: stored structures that are potentially important to a system's goals are more likely to be retrieved than irrelevant ones.

Psychologists have only begun to establish experimentally that people's analogical access is sensitive to pragmatic constraints. Part of the problem is that it is difficult to distinguish effects of goals that reflect a special pragmatic constraint from effects that can be interpreted as consequences of other general constraints involving semantic similarity and structural consistency. In general, if a representation of a structure is augmented with goal information, the augmented structure will therefore be more semantically similar to, and more structurally consistent with, other structures containing similar goal information. Nevertheless, some studies have demonstrated the importance of task goals in eliciting remindings. Seifert, McKoon, Abelson, and Ratcliff [1986] and Faries and Reiser [1988] have shown that people are sensitive to the solution-relevant aspects of previously solved problems.

Although empirical evidence is still limited, the computational argument that pragmatic constraints on retrieval are useful for narrowing the search for analogs leads us to include such constraints in the ARCS model. We view relevance to the purposes of the analogy (including explanation and argumentation, not just problem solving) as an important factor in retrieval, although not the dominant factor suggested by some AI theorists. Problems and plans have explicit purposes that should play a role in retrieval; similar pragmatic constraints could also operate in the case of stories and other structures with less specific purposes. As in the ACME mapping model, we treat pragmatic centrality as an additional pressure to semantic similarity and structural consistency. If an element of the target is relevant to the goal, the pressure of pragmatic centrality will favor retrieval of analogs that allow the important target element to be mapped.

Parallel constraint satisfaction

We propose, therefore, that retrieval of analogs from memory is determined by simultaneous satisfaction of the constraints of semantic similarity, structural consistency, and pragmatic centrality. When a target analog is presented in the form of a problem to be solved, an explanation to be given, or a conclusion to be reached, search for potentially useful source analogs in memory proceeds by searching memory for analogs that look promising for semantic, structural, and pragmatic reasons. Search is massively parallel, so that many different analogs can be simultaneously examined for potential relevance. But to prevent the system from being swamped by too many analogs for lesser relevance, search is competitive, in the sense that the retrieval of one analog tends to suppress the retrieval of other analogs. We will now describe how these ideas can be implemented computationally.

Major Characteristics

The theory of analogical retrieval is implemented in the parallel connectionists program ARCS. The major features of ARCS are presented in the following section (Thagard, Holyoak, Nelson, & Gochfeld 1990, 268–269):

ARCS (analog retrieval by constraint satisfaction) is a COMMON LISP program that retrieves analogs using multiple constraints. In brief, the program operates as follows. Retrieval is initiated from a probe structure and is intended to find structures in memory that are analogous to the probe. Search for the analogs of the probe proceeds initially using the predicates in the probe, looking for predicates that are in some degree semantically similar to them. If a predicate that is semantically similar to a predicate in the probe structure occurs in a stored structure, there is a possibility that the stored structure is analogous to the probe structure. Many stored structures, however, are likely to have some semantic overlap with the probe structure, and the principle task of ARCS is to pick out the ones that are the most relevant according to the constraints of semantic similarity, structural consistency, and pragmatic centrality. As potentially analogous structures are noticed, ARCS sets up a constraint network to compare their relevance to the probe structure. Once this constraint network has been built, ARCS uses a standard parallel connectionist relaxation algorithm to settle into a state that indicates the relative correspondence of the various stored structures to the probe structure.

Figure [3.1] provides a rough picture of how the retrieval process works. The probe structure at the bottom contains five dots corresponding to predicates used in representing the probe. Each of these predicates is linked to an associated conceptual structure, indicated by the dots outside the probe structure. Each of these concepts in turn has access to numerous other concepts that are semantically similar to it, and predicates corresponding to these concepts occur in various stored analogs S1-S5. Of these, S2 and S5 have greater semantic overlap than the others with the probe by virtue of multiple semantic links, so these two stored structures are prime candidates for analogical retrieval. However, determination of the optimal apparent analog will depend on structural and pragmatic constraints in addition to the semantic links that initially suggested possible relevance. Thus retrieval has two broad steps:

(1) finding semantically associated structures in memory,
(2) assessing these initial candidate structures in terms of the full set of constraints.

Generality of Application

Thagard, Holyoak, Nelson, and Gochfeld summarize the range of application of the ARCS system: "ARCS' data bases now include, respectively, 5 radiation problems, 5 Karla the hawk stories, 100 fables, and synopses of 25 plays" (1990, 272).

FIGURE 3.1
Probing into Long-term Memory

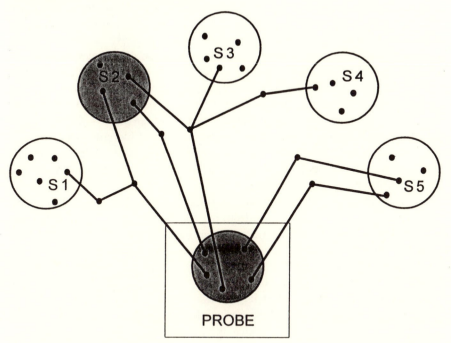

Note: This figure depicts probing from a structure into long-term memory via conceptual links. The large circles represent structures stored in memory. The dots represent concepts; the lines connect semantically similar concepts.

Source: P. Thagard, K. Holyoak, G. Nelson, and D. Gochfeld, "Analog Retrieval by Constraint Satisfaction," *Artificial Intellitgence* 46 (1990): 259–310.

WordNet Memory Structure

A fundamental source of the competence of ARCS across a range of applications is its use of the powerful WordNet electronic lexicon, as described in the following section (Thagard, Holyoak, Nelson, & Gochfeld 1990, 272–273):

In order to find concepts that are semantically similar to the concepts in a probe structure, we need to encode semantic information. ARCS' semantic structures are modeled after WordNet, an electronic lexical reference system based on psycholinguistic theories of the organization of human lexical memory [Miller, Fellbaum, Kegl, and Miller, 1988; Miller and Johnson-Laird, 1976]. In WordNet, a concept is represented by a set of synonyms, and synonym sets are organized by means of kind, part-whole, and anyonymy relations. Kind and part-whole relations are fundamental to the organization of the lexicon because they generate hierarchies. For example, a whale is a kind of cetacean, which is a kind of mammal, which is a kind of animal, which is a kind of living thing; a toe is a part of a foot, which is part of a leg, which is part of a body. WordNet now includes more than 60,000 entries, including verbs and adjectives as well as nouns. One advantage of working on such a large scale is that the differences between the kinds of lexical items becomes readily apparent. Kind and part-whole hierarchies apply well to nouns, but adjectives are primarily organized into antonymic clusters, such as that posed by the extremes wet-dry. According to the WordNet researchers, verbs have entailment hierarchies rather than part-whole hierarchies, and their kind hierarchies seem to differ from the kind hierarchies of nouns in ways that are still under investigation. The input to ARCS includes semantic information for each predicate in each structure. ARCS' semantics now include entries for more than 1200 words.

A major advantage of using WordNet is that it allows us to establish semantic structures in relative independence from the particular analogs we wish the program to retrieve, thus providing a stronger test of the model. ARCS uses the same semantic information for all its data bases. Approximately two thirds of the entries derive directly from WordNet. The WordNet entries themselves were generated from many different sources, especially dictionaries and thesauruses. Our own supplemental entries derive largely from *Roget's International Thesaurus (4th ed.)*, and *Webster's Ninth New Collegiate Dictionary*.

Here are some samples of our lexical information, for a noun, an adjective, and a verb.

ANIMAL
    SUPERORDINATES: organism living-thing
    SUBORDINATES: prey person child mammal primate reptile amphibian fish bird insect vertebrate invertebrate game
    PARTS: voice tooth tail claw-of-claw antler
    PLURAL: animals
    SYNONYMS: beast creature fauna
    ANTONYMS: plant flora
AFRAID
    SYNONYMS: afraid-of fearful dreading alarmed frightened apprehensive anxious uneasy apprehensive scared terrified worried
    ANTONYMS: unafraid confident secure
ABDICATE
    TENSES: abdicates abdicated abdicating
    SYNONYMS: resign vacate relinquish cede renounce

Because a mammal is a kind of animal, the predicate ANIMAL has MAMMAL as a subordinate and MAMMAL has ANIMAL as a superordinate. (In our terminology, if A is a kind of B, then A is a subordinate of B, and B is a superordinate of A.) WordNet is still under development, and the 1988 version we used did not include verb subordinates and superordinates that have been added to later versions. Ideally, the lists of superordinates and subordinates should include only immediate links, so that ANIMAL would be directly linked only to MAMMAL and not to PERSON. A full theory of semantic decomposition might make it possible to derive synonyms, rather than taking them as a given, but we follow WordNet in simply listing them. We have added plurals and tenses to this data base so that structures that use variants of the same predicates can be retrieved.

The WordNet-style semantic information enables ARCS to make judgments of the semantic similarity of any two predicates based on the kinds of semantic relations between them. The greatest degree of semantic similarity holds between identical predicates, with synonymy constituting a lesser degree. Still lower degrees of similarity derive from kind relations (subordinate and superordinate) and part relations. The algorithm used by ARCS to compute semantic similarity is stated below.

Psychological Validity

ARCS is viewed as a simulation of the human retrieval of relevant analogies from memory. In the following section, two tests of the closeness of the simulation between ARCS and human retrieval are described (Thagard, Holyoak, Nelson, & Gochfeld 1990, 291–298):

ARCS is intended to be a model of human cognition, so it is essential that it be consistent with the results of psychological experiments on analog retrieval. We will accordingly describe its performance in simulating the results of two sets of experiments done by Holyoak and his colleagues and by Gentner and her colleagues.

Convergence Problems

As reviewed briefly above, Holyoak and his colleagues have done a series of experiments in which the target problem to be solved concerns using an X-ray to destroy a tumor deep inside a patient [Gick and Holyoak, 1980, 1983; Holyoak and Koh, 1987] (see Duncker (1945) for the original use of the tumor problem). Simply shooting the X-ray beams at the tumor is not an acceptable solution, because the beams, if shot at sufficient intensity to destroy the tumor, will also destroy intervening healthy tissue and kill the patient. A "convergence" solution is appropriate: using multiple beams weak enough not to hurt the patient, but aimed from several directions so that they converge on the tumor with enough intensity to destroy it. Very few subjects discover this strategy on their own, but they are more likely to formulate the convergence solution if they have first been provided with an analog. In the various experiments, analogs have been used with markedly different degrees of similarity to the tumor problem, and subjects' ability to retrieve them from memory and notice their relevance, without any hint from the experimenter, has varied accordingly.

We cannot simulate the relevant experiments directly, since that would require constructing the full knowledge base of the various subjects and incorporating different stored analogs. However, since we are interested in the relative retrievability of the different analogs, we can contrive a data base consisting of all of the analogs and see which ones ARCS prefers to retrieve. Our data base accordingly consists of the following five structures:

— the laser problem (version 1), in which a laser beam is used to fuse a filament in a lightbulb by convergence from several directions, avoiding breaking the bulb (high semantic similarity, high structural consistency);
— the laser problem (version 2), in which a laser beam is used to fuse a filament in a lightbulb, but where convergence is required because the original beam is too weak, not because of the danger of destroying the bulb (high semantic similarity, low structural consistency);
— the ultrasound problem (version 1), in which an ultrasound device is used to split apart a filament in a lightbulb by convergence from several directions, avoiding breaking the bulb (low semantic similarity, high structural consistency);
— the ultrasound problem (version 2), in which an ultrasound device is used to split apart a filament in a lightbulb, but where convergence is required because the original beam is too weak, not because of the danger of destroying the bulb (low semantic similarity, low structural consistency);
— the fortress problem (version 2), in which an army succeeds in attacking a fortress by dispersing its troops and attacking it from multiple directions; here the convergence solution is necessary because a frontal assault will lead to the destruction of the army.

The first four of the above problems provide a factorial manipulation of degree of semantic similarity and degree of structural consistency, and their relative accessibility was accessed in a single experiment by Holyoak and Koh (1987). The fifth problem has been used in many other experiments [Catrambone and Holyoak, 1990; Gick and Holyoak, 1980, 1983; Spencer and Weisberg, 1986]. To test the relative retrievability of these analogs, we translated the materials used by Holyoak and his colleagues into predicate calculus and added the relevant semantic information concerning the predicates used. An English version of the tumor problem is the following:

Suppose you are a doctor faced with a patient who has a malignant tumor in his stomach. It is impossible to operate on the patient, but unless the tumor is destroyed the patient will die. There is a kind of ray that can be used to destroy the tumor. If the rays reach the tumor all at once at a sufficiently high intensity, the tumor will be destroyed. Unfortunately, at this intensity, the healthy tissue that the rays pass through on the way to the tumor will also be destroyed. At lower intensities the rays are harmless to healthy tissue, but they will not affect the tumor either. What type of procedure might be used to destroy the tumor with the rays, and at the same time avoid destroying the healthy tissue?

WordNet-style concepts were constructed for the 72 predicates used in the probe problem and in the five stored structures.

We then used the tumor problem as a probe into the data base containing the other five problems. ARCS created a network of 100 units and 1104 links, and took 95 cycles to settle.

The results correspond quite well with the degree of retrievability observed in the psychological experiments. [Table 3.1] compares (1) the percent of subjects in the experiments who were able to generate the convergence solution without any hint with (2) the activation of the unit representing the correspondence between the probe tumor problem and the stored analog. For the four versions of the lightbulb problems, the order of activations corresponds to the empirical measure of accessibility in the Holyoak and Koh (1987) experiments. Similarly, Holyoak and Thagard (1989) used the ACME program to simulate post-retrieval mapping performance using data from this same experiment.

The relative activation of the fortress problem is worse than the empirical measure would apparently predict. However, this measure was obtained with different

TABLE 3.1
Comparison of ARCS Results with
Retrievability of Radiation Problem Analogs

	Percentage of Subjects Achieving Solution	Asymptotic Activation of ARCS Unit
Laser problem (fragile glass)	69	0.22
Ultrasound problem (fragile glass)	38	0.15
Laser problem (insufficient intensity)	33	0.11
Ultrasound problem (insufficient intensity	13	0.05
Fortress problem	30	−0.12

Source: P. Thagard, K. Holyoak, G. Nelson, and D. Gochfeld, "Analog Retrieval by Constraint Satisfaction," *Artificial Intelligence* 46 (1990): 259–310. Reprinted with permission of Elsevier Science Publishers and the author.

subjects in different experiments than was the data for the other four problems, so precise comparisons are unwarranted. Also, subjects in the actual experiments using the fortress problems had only one of the lightbulb problems stored in memory, whereas ARCS had all of them in competition.

"Karla the Hawk" Stories

Gentner and her colleagues have performed a series of experiments concerning the retrievability of a number of similar stories, and ARCS has also been used to simulate these results. [Figure 3.2] gives the English versions of one set of stories from Rattermann and Gentner (1987). . . . Ratterman and Gentner first had subjects read a list of 32 stories, including 20 crucial stories such as "Karla the Hawk." Then subjects were given a series of probe stories, including one of the four alternative stories listed in [Figure 3.2], and were asked to write down any story they were reminded of by the probe. (In Gentner's terminology, "target" corresponds to our "probe," and "base" corresponds to our "source.") The four versions manipulated the similarity of the probe and source story. The "literal-similarity" and "mere-appearance" conditions were high in overall semantic similarity, whereas the "true-analogy" and "false-analogy" conditions were low in overall similarity. The literal-similarity and true-analogy conditions preserve the pattern of causal relations in the probe, whereas the mere-appearance and false-analogy conditions did not. Thus the design provides a factorial manipulation of degree of semantic similarity and degree of structural consistency at the level of causal relations.

As in the case of the convergence problems, it is impractical to simulate the actual knowledge of subjects in Ratterman and Gentner's experiment. As a surrogate for general memory, we used the fables data base. . . . Because many of the 100 fables concern animals, as do the Rattermann and Gentner stories, they serve as excellent distractors for the probe story. We did four retrieval simulations, using the same parameters as in the simulations involving the tumor problem. . . . As [Table 3.2] indicates, ARCS' simulation corresponded well with the results of the psychological experiments. Each probe story retrieved the "Karla the Hawk" story, but the retrievability of that story as measured by the number of fables that were better retrieved varied inversely with the number of subjects recalling the story in the Rattermann and Gentner experiment. That is, the greater the percentage of the subjects retrieving the "Karla the Hawk" story using the probe of a particular type, the better the story did in relation to the fables also stored in memory. The ordering of activations of the units shows a small reversal for the true-analogy and false-analogy case relative to ordering of the retrieval percentages obtained by Rattermann and Gentner, but we view this as an artifact of there being so many more fables activated in the true-analogy case than in the false-analogy case.

FIGURE 3.2
English Versions of "Karla the Hawk" Stories

Base Story

Karla, an old hawk, lived at the top of a tall oak tree. One afternoon, she saw a hunter on the ground with a bow and some crude arrows that had no feathers. The hunter took aim and shot at the hawk but missed. Karla knew the hunter wanted her feathers so she glided down to the hunter and offered to give him a few. The hunter was so grateful that he pledged never to shoot at a hawk again. He went off and shot deer instead.

Literal Similarity

Once there was an eagle named Zerdia who nested on a rocky cliff. One day she saw a sportsman coming with a crossbow and some bolts that had no feathers. The sportsman attacked but the bolts missed. Zerdia realized that the sportsman wanted her tailfeathers so she flew down and donated a few of her tailfeathers to the sportsman. The sportsman was pleased. He promised never to attack eagles again.

True Analogy

Once there was a small country called Zerdia that learned to make the world's smartest computer.

One day Zerdia was attacked by its warlike neighbor, Gagrach. But the missiles were badly aimed and the attack failed. The Zerdian government realized that Gagrach wanted Zerdian computers so it offered to sell some of its computers to the country. The government of Gagrach was very pleased. It promised never to attack Zerdia again.

Mere Appearance

Once there was an eagle named Zerdia who donated a few of her tailfeathers to a sportsman so he would promise never to attack eagles.

One day Zerdia was nesting high on a rocky cliff when she saw the sportsman coming with a crossbow. Zerdia flew down to meet the man, but he attacked and felled her with a single bolt. As she fluttered to the ground Zerdia realized that the bolt had her own tailfeathers on it.

False Analogy

Once there was a small country called Zerdia that learned to make the world's smartest computer. Zerdia sold one of its supercomputers to its neighbor, Gagrach, so Gagrach promised never to attack Zerdia.

But one day Zerdia was overwhelmed by a surprise attack from Gagrach. As it capitulated the crippled government of Zerdia realized that the attacker's missiles had been guided by Zerdian supercomputers.

Source: P. Thagard, K. Holyoak, G. Nelson, and D. Gochfeld, "Analog Retrieval by Constraint Satisfaction," *Artificial Intelligence* 46 (1990): 259–310. Reprinted with permission of Elsevier Science Publishers.

TABLE 3.2

Comparison of ARCS Simulations with "Karla the Hawk" Experiment (Rattermann and Gentner [48])

	Percentage of Subjects Retrieving Story	Rank of "Karla" Unit	Asymptotic Activation of "Karla" Unit
Lateral symmetry	58	1 of 68	0.67
Mere appearance	45	9 of 59	−0.17
True analogy	18	9 of 61	−0.27
False analogy	8	16 of 29	−0.11

Note: The percentages are inferred from a graph; the actual numbers were not reported by Rattermann and Gentner. By "Karla" unit we mean the unit representing the correspondence between the probe story and the "Karla the Hawk" story. In the rank column, "1 of 68" means that there were 67 fables activated in addition to the Karla story and the "Karla" unit had the highest activation.

Source: P. Thagard, K. Holyoak, G. Nelson, and D. Gochfeld, "Analog Retrieval by Constraint Satisfaction," *Artificial Intelligence* 46 (1990): 294. Reprinted with permission of Elsevier Science Publishers.

The results of Rattermann and Gentner (1987) appear to show effects of both semantic similarity and structural consistency. The latter effect reveals itself in the apparent advantage of the literal-similarity condition over the mere-appearance condition, and the advantage of the true-analogy over the false-analogy condition. Although these differences fell short of statistical significance, each of these two trends was replicated in two separate experiments [Gentner and Landers, 1984; Rattermann and Gentner, 1987], and in one experiment the advantage of the true analogy relative to the false analogy was significant [Gentner and Landers, 1985]. Note that pragmatic centrality plays no role in the "Karla the Hawk" simulations, since the stories are not problems, explanations, or arguments. We agree with Gentner (1989) (in contrast, for example, to Hammond (1986)) that semantic similarity is the most important constraint on analog retrieval, although we maintain that structural and pragmatic constraints are also used when such information is available.

Computational Scope

In addition to the evaluation of ARCS as a model of human cognition, the computational power of the system is considered. The evaluation of the computational scope of ARCS is summarized in the following section (Thagard, Holyoak, Nelson, & Gochfeld 1990, 298):

ARCS is thus consistent with some major psychological experiments on analog retrieval, and therefore gains some credibility as a cognitive model. However, it is also important to do computational experiments to determine what happens in data bases in which the presence of many potential source analogs raises the danger of either retrieving too many not-so-relevant analogs or requiring too much computation to select out the more relevant ones.

To provide experimental answers to questions concerning how well ARCS scales up, we constructed two large data bases consisting of 100 fables and 24 synopses of Shakespeare's plays. Tests on the first data base show that ARCS is capable of screening the wheat from the chaff in a data base of many complex structures, whereas tests on the second data base show that it is capable of handling even more complex structures: the fables average about 22 propositions per structure whereas the plays average about 55.

Evaluation Results

The following conclusion is drawn from the research evaluation of the ARCS system (Thagard, Holyoak, Nelson, & Gochfeld 1990, 305–306):

We conclude on the basis of the above evaluation that ARCS provides a psychologically plausible and computationally powerful model of memory for analogs. People retrieve complex structures by simultaneously applying semantic, structural, and pragmatic constraints, with the semantic constraints being most crucial for initiating the probe process.

Relationship to Analogical Thinking

In the following section, the place of ARCS is sketched in an overall computational model of analogical thinking (Thagard, Holyoak, Nelson, & Gochfeld 1990, 306–307):

ARCS is only part of a full model of analogy. Retrieval should blend naturally into mapping, so that when the retrieval system has selected a possible analog, the mapping system can go to work to determine in more detail how well the two structures correspond. Our mapping program ACME (Holyoak and Thagard, 1989) uses similar principles to ARCS, and preliminary tests show that passing ARCS results directly to ACME greatly facilitates ACME's ability to fill in a complete mapping. ACME is not so dependent on semantic similarity as ARCS and can fill in the mappings of elements with no semantic overlap.

After an analogy system has performed retrieval and mapping, it still needs to transfer the results of the analogy for the appropriate problem-solving, explanatory, argumentative, or evocative purpose. At this point, the goals of the system should be more important than anything else, although semantics and structural consistency many also contribute. Thus in our view all three constraints — semantic, structural, *and* pragmatic — are important to all three stages of analogy: retrieval, mapping and transfer. As [Table 3.3] summarizes, however, the importance of the different constraints to the different stages is hypothesized to vary, with semantics paramount for retrieval, structural constraints paramount for mapping, and pragmatics paramount for transfer.

TABLE 3.3
Summary of Hypothesized Importance of Different
Constraints to Different Stages of Analogical Thinking

	Semantic	Isomorphism	Pragmatic
Retrieval (ARCS)	Very	Yes	Yes
Mapping (ACME)	Yes	Very	Yes
Transfer	Yes	Yes	Very

Note: Here Yes means that the constraint is important, and Very means that the constraint is very important.

Source: P. Thagard, K. Holyoak, G. Nelson, and D. Gochfeld, "Analog Retrieval by Constraint Satisfaction," *Artificial Intelligence* 46 (1990): 259–310. Reprinted with permission of Elsevier Science Publishers.

A fourth stage of analogy use is learning: if analogy proves to be useful, various strategies can be applied to learn from the success (e.g., by schematizing the two analogs and by forming rules about how to use such schemas). Our earlier system PI (Holyoak and Thagard, 1989) has such capabilities. Another attractive feature of PI is that it does both rule-based and analogical problem solving within the same cognitive architecture. We see no point in making a sharp contrast between rule-based and analogical (case-based) problem solving, since a system that approximates the power of human performance should gracefully incorporate both mechanisms. We are currently developing a cognitive architecture that integrates the constraint-satisfaction methods of ARCS and ACME with a rule-based problem solver. The amalgamation of a rule-based problem solver and our constraint-satisfaction programs reflects our view that connectionist and traditional AI approaches belong to a continuum of complementary computational methods.

Commentary

Thagard, Holyoak, Nelson, and Gochfeld (1990) have made an important initial contribution to the determination of the conditions that control retrieval of analogs in computers and in humans. It is reasonable that, among other constraints, semantic constraints are paramount in the selection of possible candidates and that isomorphic and pragmatic constraints further limit the selection process.

These researchers make an even stronger contribution to a general theory of analogical thinking, having sketched the relative contribution of their triadic constraints to the sequential stages of analogical thinking: retrieval, mapping, and problem solving. There are, however, formidable difficulties in the further development of a general theory of analogical thinking.

The chief difficulty is that whereas the semantic constraint can largely be met by an electronic lexicon such as WordNet, the pragmatic constraint must often depend on the input of human judgment to the system. As with D. B. Lenat's AM System, judgment about what is interesting, relevant, creative, appropriate, etc., is not a fixed algorithmic product. The human cognitive system is responsive to subtle changes in context that make analogy more or less close, facilitating or impeding, respectively, the closeness of reasoning.

ARTIFICIAL INTELLIGENCE AND ANALOGICAL REASONING

Conceptual Components of Analogical Reasoning

In "Computational Approaches to Analogical Reasoning: A Comparative Analysis," an abstract component model of the processes of analogical reasoning that is applicable to both artificial intelligence and human cognition is presented (Hall, 1989, 43):

This framework gives abstract process components that a relatively complete picture of analogical reasoning, computational or otherwise, would include:

1) *recognition* of a candidate analogous source, given a target description,
2) *elaboration* of an analogical mapping between source and target domains, possibly including a set of analogous inferences,
3) *evaluation* of the mapping and inferences in some context of use, including justification, repair, or extension of the mapping,
4) and *consolidation* of the outcome of the analogy so that its results can be usefully reinstated in other contexts.

These components provide a conceptual organization for comparing computational approaches to analogy.

With the four-component process model used as a guide, 16 computational studies of analogical reasoning are compared. These studies are summarized with respect to component processes of recognition and elaboration in the following account (Hall 1989, 113–114):

Contributions of individual studies to processes of recognition and elaboration

Study	Recognition	Elaboration
Evans (1968) ANALOGY	given	object type and rule components restrict object and rule mappings; relational mapping enabled by a fixed vocabulary of substitutions
Becker (1973) JCM	associative memory of schemata indexed by general concepts	kernel predicates map identically; node mismatch weighted by a linear combination of salience estimates; best candidate maximizes match score and schema confidence, minimizes cost
Kling (1971) ZORBA	given	partial mapping over theorem statements is extended by a type-restricted best-first search
Munyer (1981)	source formulas and derivations indexed by functional containment	extends unification through bottom-up, competitive reinforcement of a global mapping; requires consistent mappings at boundaries of the source derivation
Greiner (1988) NLAG	given a hint, generate a source problem and find an abstraction for solving it	find a target instance of the abstraction, inferring residual conjectures as needed
Brown (1977)	source domain given by tutorial context	incrementally extend a type-restricted mapping; map target problem into a source problem and solve it
McDermott (1979) ANA	manipulate target cues to trigger method indices; anticipate method failures	map source into existing or "stipulated" target objects; extend mapping to cover method subgoals

Carbonell (1983) ARIES	solution paths are indexed by states and constraints; a similarity metric screens candidate source sequences	map source and target sequences
Carbonell (1986)	similar initial reasoning triggers retrieval of a source derivation from dynamic memory	map source and target sequences
Simpson (1985) MEDIATOR	collect source remindings by traversing an episodic memory for plans and failures; select a source candidate that preserves an invariance hierarchy	mapping is distributed across index tests; align identical norm slots
Winston (1978) FOX	a simile is given by a tutor or conjectured by the learner	prefer existing transfer frames, salient properties of the source, properties that are prototypical of the target class, or properties that continue the instructional context
Hobbs (1983) DIANA	a source schema is triggered by the appearance of target predicates	resolution of discourse problems aligns source and target concepts
Dyer (1983) BORRIS	target planning failures trigger retrieval of a source narrative from dynamic memory	map narrative elements through a common planning
Winston (1986) MACBETH	recognize source by bottom-up voting through exhaustive type indexing; index rules by actors, acts, and objects	map a priori important relations before lower level relations
Burstein (1986) CARL	given source domain, a target example and reasoning context triggers retrieval of a source abstraction from dynamic memory	top-down relational mapping includes objects only as needed; can map non-identical relations
Pirolli (1985)	selects prior example under production control; spreading activation	mapping productions (some are learned) align code template components

	retrieves declarative memory structures	
Kedar-Cabelli (1985)	select a source instance and plan (not described); explain why the source instance satisfies the purpose	map the source explanation and plan to the target instance

The set of computational studies in analogical reasoning is summarized with respect to the process components of evaluation and consolidation in the following section (Hall 1989, 114–115):

Contributions of individual studies to processes of evaluation and consolidation

Study	Evaluation	Consolidation
Evans (1968) ANALOGY	drop unmatched relations and prefer candidates that preserve most source relations (A:B)	proposes rule proceduralization and generalization
Becker (1973) JCM	unmapped source kernels are treated as subgoals to be confirmed	store the target interpretation; weight adjustments introduce variables, drop conditions, and estimate a schema's worth
Kling (1971) ZORBA	pass target clauses to a separate resolution theorem prover	none
Munyer (1981)	implicit planning uses analogy as an evaluation function; explicit planning detects skewed analogies and finds plan repair steps; both succeed when a logically valid derivation is found	record the target derivation; generalize formulas and derivational sequences; delete redundant or unsuccessful derivations
Greiner (1988) NLAG	verify that inferred facts solve the target problem, are consistent with existing knowledge, and are acceptable to the user	add inferred facts to the domain theory

Brown (1977)	lift the source solution into the target domain; confirm transferred justifications, patching "bugs" as necessary	add successful descriptions, plans, justification, and code to the target domain repertoire
McDermott (1979) ANA	environment and user feedback confirms method expectations or signals method errors; repair by subgoaling on failure or selecting an alternate method	builds error detection and recovery productions; adds target instantiation of successful method production
Carbonell (1983) ARIES	MEA in T-space reduces differences between source and target sequences	store target solution sequence; generalize operator sequences; tune similarity metric and difference table; cluster over T-space failures
Carbonell (1986)	check justifications for source steps in target description; reconsider alternative source steps or prior failures; monitor a perseverance threshold	update case memory with target solution; generalize target and source traces; justification points identify instances for learning search heuristics; decompose traces into general plan components
Simpson (1985) MEDIATOR	verify the source classification and plan preconditions in target; confirm plan predictions with user; remediate failures	memory update installs, inserts, and generalizes episodic structures
Winston (1978) FOX	check for violations of known target properties, confirm existing justification frames, or ask the tutor	transfer properties; construct transfer, justification, and typical-instance frames; conjecture additional properties or new similes
Hobbs (1983) DIANA	preserve contextual coherence and satisfy pragmatic constraints	target schemata are extended; metaphors tire and die with repeated use
Dyer (1983) BORRIS MORRIS	find a coherent interpretation of the target narrative; confirm plan-based predictions	augment the target interpretation; reorganize existing memory structures to maintain discriminable access to the target narrative

Winston (1986) MACBETH	analogical inferences are confirmed directly by further analogies, by abductive inference, or by the teacher	record the target case; build general inference rules; augment rules to censor exceptions; index original case with rule
Burstein (1986) CARL	discard unsupported inferences; tutor gives feedback and corrections; multiple analogies correct misconceptions	integrate multiple causal abstractions in the target domain
Pirolli (1985)	check inferred components against the target specification; test target code in the LISP environment; repair or abandon the current analogy	proceduralization and composition build general productions which supplant structural analogies
Kedar-Cabelli (1985)	justify explanatory inferences for target; replace structural attributes or plan steps as necessary	find a common explanatory structure for the refined concept

Process Component:
Recognition of a Candidate Analogy

The construction of an analogy between a source and a target is initiated with a search for potentially applicable knowledge contained in the source. The search is typically guided by selective constraints, as discussed in the following passage (Hall 1989, 96):

Given an unfamiliar situation (the *target*), how does a reasoner connect this new situation with one or more familiar situations (*sources*) contained in a store of previous experience? From a computational perspective, search is implicated and an organization is usually imposed on the store of previous experience to help constrain search for a candidate source. From a cognitive perspective, a reasoner attends to familiar aspects of the target and uses these aspects to retrieve appropriate experiences from memory. By allowing partial similarity between target and candidate sources, a central problem of recognition is to impose constraints on the retrieval process but still allow recognition of analogically related sources. For example, strict organizational criteria that suppress tenuously related candidates might not allow recognition of relatively abstract inter-domain analogies.

The following section compares computational studies with respect to how recognition constraints are established or imposed (Hall 1989, 96):

The most effective but least ambitious solution to constraining recognition is to give the reasoner a source analog. Some studies do this as a simplifying assumption (e.g., Evans (1968), Kling (1971), or Pirolli and Anderson (1985)), while others give a hint about the source and rely on supporting mechanisms to complete recognition. For example, Kedar-Cabelli (1985) gives the learning purpose, the to-be-learned concept, and a target instance. The system then selects a prototypical source instance and a plan for using that instance to achieve the given purpose. Using a similar approach, Greiner (1985) gives an initial mapping (a hint) between source and target concepts, and then finds a source instantiation and an abstraction for solving it. Both approaches use the relation of an abstraction (or plan) to a source instance during later stages of analogical reasoning. Brown's (1977) reduction analogies, Winston's (1978) simile-based instruction, and Burstein's (1986) integration of multiple analogical models each place analogy in a tutorial context. In all three cases, the reasoner uses a hint and the ongoing tutoring context to recognize salient aspects of the source. For example, Burstein gives the analogy (e.g., a variable is like a box) and examples of its use, and CARL retrieves a source abstraction (e.g., a causal model of containment) to extend the analogy.

A prominent method of controlling constraint is indexing, as described below (Hall 1989, 97–98):

Without giving the analogy directly, other source candidates compete for attention and require an organization that restricts their number. This organization is generally an indexing scheme that enforces selective retrieval. The reviewed studies use three general approaches: nonselective indexing, task-specific indexing, and task-independent indexing. In each, the question is what to choose as indices into the store of candidate sources. Choosing an indexing scheme makes an explicit commitment to the kinds of analogies that can be recognized.

Nonselective indexing schemes approximate an associative memory for candidate sources. For example, Becker (1973) indexes candidate schemata through generic concept nodes, while Munyer (1981) indexes formulas around instances of functional containment. Each approach promises extensive search in a memory with relatively primitive organization. In practice, each applies additional constraints to the search process: Becker insists that mapped kernels occur in an appropriate position in the schema, and Munyer requires consistent formula mappings at either end of a candidate derivation. In both cases, recognition returns a set of candidate source analogs, and one (or several) are selected during elaboration and evaluation. For example, Munyer suggests an agenda control mechanism prioritized by the "degree of certainty" for competing analogical views.

Task-specific indexing schemes select distinguished elements of the representation and make an a priori commitment that these elements predict future contexts of use for the source. Winston's (1980) "classification-exploiting hypothesizing" resembles this scheme, although he mentions using relational indexing in the bottom-up voting mechanism. His later work (Winston, 1982) indexes acquired rules by the types of actors, acts, and objects found in their right-hand sides. Extracting type cues from the target problem, Winston retrieves sources which make predictions about those types. McDermott (1978) uses a similar strategy when indexing source method productions by types of objects and actions. As with nonselective approaches, both studies include further constraints on recognition. Winston (1980) weights his voting scheme in negative proportion to source concept prevalence and in positive proportion to the contextual salience of the target concept. McDermott, on the other hand, generates taxonomic variants of the target cue to make contact with method indices. In each case, differential focus on target elements refines cue extraction, allowing the reasoner to influence the recognition process by manipulating elements of the target description. Although task-specific indexing and cue extraction prove effective for the problems solved in these studies (e.g., painting or washing tables), these methods may not extend across more heterogeneous tasks and may not recognize more abstract analogical similarity between target and source domains.

Task-independent indexing schemes select more abstract representational elements for indices that organize memory. Carbonell's (1981, 1982) "invariance hierarchy" over semantic categories is an example of this approach. Examining metaphors and analogies in different domains, Carbonell ranks semantic categories by decreasing order of invariant transfer. The resulting hierarchy specifies that goals, plans and causal structure are usually preserved in an analogical mapping. Carbonell argues that this invariant hierarchy is important for recognizing analogies since memory can be organized around (i.e., indices are based on) precisely the knowledge structures that are likely to transfer without variation when reasoning by analogy. Thus, recognition proceeds by extracting goals, plans, or causal structure from the target and using these as indices into a memory for candidate sources. For example, Carbonell (1983) organizes a memory for solution sequences in ARIES around state descriptions (initial and goal states) and constraints, and then uses a similarity metric based on the same information to select among recognized candidates. Dyer also (1983) uses this indexing scheme to organize memory around instances of planning failures (TAUs). Planning difficulties in a target narrative serve as retrieval cues for recognizing adages and analogous narrative episodes. Likewise, Simpson (1985) recognizes analogous cases by comparing a target description with generalized episodes in a memory organized hierarchically around problem types and planning information. Traversing indices in episodic memory structures guides the recognition process through increasingly specific comparisons ending with retrieval of candidate cases. By indexing and retrieving over task-independent semantic categories,

these approaches can support recognition and retrieval of genuinely novel
metaphors or analogies.

Of these three indexing schemes, the task-independent approach might be preferred since it anticipates retrieval of useful source candidates and clearly allows
recognition of analogies where target and source content are markedly different.
. . . Also, as argued by Schank (1982), Dyer (1983), and Kolodner (1983a,
1983b), these approaches appear consistent with human studies of episodic memory organization and retrieval. On the other hand, task-independent indexing
schemes could make overly strong a priori commitments to the utility of source
situations, preventing access in some useful but unexpected contexts. This is
especially true when the target is completely novel, since the reasoner may not be
able to extract cues required for recognition of a useful analogy from a memory
organized around abstract semantic categories. Evidence from studies of human
analogical access (Gentner, 1987) suggests that recognizing an analogical source
may depend on different principles than those that determine elaboration and
evaluation. At present, it seems likely that analogical retrieval depends on interactions between several factors: what the reasoner attends to in the target situation, what is available in the store of source experiences, and the degree to which
the reasoning context during recognition matches the encoding context for a
stored source. These tradeoffs are open research questions for computational
studies. As psychological models of memory organization and retrieval become
more explicit, computational approaches to recognition may benefit; the converse
may also be true.

Process Component:
Elaboration of Analogical Mapping

Elaboration is the process of mapping an analogy between source
domain and target domain. In the elaborative process, constraints are exer-
cised to yield an effective analogical mapping. Methods of constraints can
be grouped as relational, semantic, and contextual, as described below
(Hall 1989, 100–101, italics added):

*The first class of preferences considers representations of the source and target,
asking what aspects of those representations should be preserved.* The most general approach, as evident in many studies, is to preserve the relational structure of
the source representation. For example, Brown (1977) maps predicates from
source to target domains only if those predicates have the same type and their
arguments have a type-compatible mapping. With similar effect, Munyer
(1981) uses a bottom-up approach in which local maps between arguments compete to reinforce predicate mappings higher in the representational network. In
both cases, the relational structure of a source representation is preserved in
the analogy mapping if a corresponding structure can be found in the target

representation. This approach is also found in algorithms for computing inductive summaries over instances (e.g., Hayes-Roth, 1978) and has been studied systematically by Falkenhainer (1986, 1987) as a computation realization of Gentner's structure-mapping theory (Gentner, 1983).

The second class of preferences focuses on semantic categories of source and target knowledge, asking what semantic structures are commonly preserved in analogies and metaphors. These preferences range from task-specific restrictions to preserving more general informational categories in the analogical mapping. Evans' (1968) restriction of a one-to-one mapping of rule components and Pirolli and Anderson's (1985) compilation of mapping rules are examples of task-specific semantic preferences. Winston's promotion of salient source properties when comprehending similes (Winston, 1978) or his preference for salient relations (e.g., cause or enablement relations) in importance-dominated matching (Winston, 1980) are intermediate along this continuum. Carbonell's invariance hierarchy (1981, 1982) and Simpson's (1985) use of that hierarchy to organize memory and direct elaboration are examples of the most general preference for semantic categories. Whereas the first class of mapping preferences preserve relational structure in source and target descriptions, this class promotes semantic categories deemed important for the analogy a priori.

The third class of preferences focuses on the contextual relevance of mapped material, asking which relational or semantic structures to preserve within the current reasoning context. Since an arbitrarily large collection of facts might be known of the source or target, some mechanism must focus on those facts which are important at the moment. Contextual relevance is a broad concept, and takes different forms in the studies reviewed here. For example, Burstein (1986) uses a tutorial context to select among alternative relational abstractions in the source domains. Also arguing for contextual constraints, Kedar-Cabelli (1985) uses a to-be-learned concept and its stated purpose (e.g., drinking hot liquids) to focus elaboration on explanatory inferences used with a source instance of the concept. Perhaps the strongest adherent to contextual relevance, Hobbs (1983) argues that resolving discourse problems in context finds a coherent metaphorical interpretation.

It is pointed out that although these classes of constraints, as separately conceived, have been the objects of contention, harmony can be established by viewing them in an integrative framework (Hall 1989, 101, italics added):

In isolation, these three preference classes for elaborating an analogical mapping may seem incompatible. For example, relying solely on a preference for preserving semantic categories, a reasoner might attempt to map isolated and potentially irrelevant source goals, plans, or causal relations. These could be suppressed by a mapping strategy that preferred maximally coherent (or "systematic"

[Gentner (1983)]) relational structures. In contrast, relying solely on a preference for relational structure, a reasoner might fail to map attribute-level information that is critical for achieving some goal. These and other arguments are levelled in detail by Holyoak (1985) and Gentner (1987) and are relevant for computational research.

From an integrative viewpoint, constraints provided by all three preference classes contribute to processes of analogical reasoning. When recognition and evaluation are considered as pre- and post-processes to elaboration, many of the more strident contrasts between these approaches fall away. For example, contextual constraints on recognition help to restrict the relational structures available for mapping, while evaluation processes give a posteriori force to a preference for semantic categories. *Since these categories tend to be represented as higher-order relational structures, the more parsimonious preference for preserving relational structure within elaboration may be a tenable approach, provided that contextual and semantic constraints surround the mapping process.*

In the elaborative process, inferential reasoning between source and target may range from simple mathematical confirmations — as in proportional analogies — to complex exploratory and hypothesis testing behavior — as in scientific discovery (Hesse 1963) and as in personal problem solving. In the personal problem solving found in the PLATO Dilemma Counseling System (Wagman 1980, 1984, 1988; Wagman & Kerber 1980), an analogous match is sought from a set of specific case dilemma solutions (source) to a troubling problem (target), as described below (Hall 1989, 101–102):

Comparing different approaches to analogy, elaboration of a mapping between target and source domains is clearly a process of varying complexity. In some studies, finding a mapping between target and source descriptions directly achieves the purpose of the analogy. For example, Evans' (1968) ANALOGY system generates a set of generalized rule candidates, choosing the one that best preserves a one-to-one, type-consistent mapping between source figures. Similar descriptions apply to most psychological studies of proportional analogies (e.g., Sternberg, 1977) and comparison-based theories of metaphor comprehension (e.g., Malgady and Johnson, 1980). In contrast, other studies describe elaboration as an active, incremental process. For example, Carbonell (1983, 1986) starts with a partial mapping over problem specifications (e.g., states and constraints) and then enters a complicated search space of plan transformations or replayed derivational steps to find a solution for the target problem. The repairs described by McDermott (1979) and Burstein (1986) or the justification for a new case described by Kedar-Cabelli (1985) suggest similar complexity when elaborating an effective analogy.

Simple, relatively homogenous correspondence as an end in itself supports a limited view of analogy: analogical comparisons finds a mapping which renders two superficially dissimilar situations virtually identical. In this view, the real work of analogy is in elaborating a consistent mapping, and analogical inference is either missing or given a limited role. *In contrast, more complex views of elaboration see analogy as an open-ended, experimental process. An elaborated mapping supports analogical inferences from a well-understood source domain into a less familiar target domain. These inferences are hypotheses that must be verified in the target domain, giving rise to an experimental interplay between elaboration and evaluation.*

Process Component: Evaluation of the Analogy

In the evaluative process, mechanisms that confirm the validity or usefulness of the elaborated analogy are required. A number of confirmation procedures are described in the following account (Hall 1989, 103–104):

The plausibility of analogical inferences can be confirmed by consulting prototypical expectations of the target domain or verifying the usefulness of inferences in some ongoing reasoning process. In either case, evaluation tests predictions about the target domain. As an example of confirmation using target expectations, Winston (1978) "filters" inferred target properties by checking that they fill slots or have values found in a "typical" target instance. In Winston's later work (1982), abductive reasoning verifies an analogical inference when its consequences are known in the target domain or provided by a tutor. In both cases, existing knowledge of the target is used to confirm predictions from the source domain.

More ambitious evaluative strategies weigh the problem solving utility of analogical inferences. For example, Carbonell's (1983) transformational analogy mechanism uses a similarity metric to select T-operators which incrementally transform a source solution sequence into a target solution sequence. Features used in this metric (e.g., comparisons of states or path constraints) encode knowledge of desirable or undesirable solution forms in the target domain. In a more general deductive framework, Greiner's (1985) NLAG must prove that an analogical conjecture is useful for solving the target problem. As an alternative to task-specific knowledge of the target domain, Burstein (1986) uses critical interactions between CARL and a tutor to collect feedback on analogy-driven solutions that includes corrections for wrong answers. In each approach, the success of an analogical inference in reaching a target solution is used to evaluate the analogy.

Justification mechanisms constitute important methods in the evaluative process, as described below (Hall 1989, 104):

Taken in isolation, a fact or action suggested by an analogical inference may be plausible, but the reasons supporting that fact in the source domain may not be plausible when evaluated in the target domain. A common solution is to map source justifications of analogical inferences into the target domain and then to establish their validity. A justification gives a representational description of the "reasons" which support an inference or action in some domain. Becker (1973) gives an early example of this approach by collecting facts which justify a "motivated" analogical mapping. This motivation is to apply a schema in his prediction paradigm, and justifying facts are unmapped source kernels in either side of the schema (e.g., antecedent kernels in a forward application). Somewhat more direct, Winston's (1978) justification frames explicitly capture those aspects of a target description which must be present for a known analogy (i.e., a transfer frame) to be useful. For example, a justification frame for an analogy between a table and a cube to be used for a common purpose (e.g., to eat or write) might record that both target and source objects must be of medium size, have a flat top, and be level. Using functional justifications is extended by Winston et al. (1983) and used to good purpose by Kedar-Cabelli (1985). In purpose-directed analogy, an explanatory justification generated in the source domain (e.g., the structural reasons why a ceramic cup can be used to drink hot liquids) both confirms and constrains analogous reasoning in the target.

Replaying justifications is central to some computational studies of analogy. For example, Brown (1977) represents plan justifications as collections of assertions which relate steps in a solution plan to facts about the task domain found in a goal description. After generating a justified source solution, these assertions must be confirmed when the candidate solution is "inverse-mapped" into the target domain. If justifications cannot be confirmed, further elaboration of the existing analogy or introduction of a new analogy are attempted. Carbonell's derivational analogy method (1986) also replays justifications, stored as part of a derivational trace of decisions made when solving a source problem (e.g., programming quicksort in PASCAL). Given an analogous target problem (e.g., programming quicksort in LISP), the reasons for choosing among actions in the source derivation must be confirmed or replaced by alternative reasons for the derivational analogy to succeed.

The result of the evaluative process may be the detection of a faulty analogical bridge between source and target domains. The problem of repairing faulty analogies is discussed in the following account (Hall 1989, 105, italics added):

A number of studies use multiple analogies to repair inappropriate analogical inferences. For example, Burstein's (1986) CARL integrates multiple analogical models (e.g., physical containment and human memory) to repair incorrect predictions about simple assignment statements. Among the variety of studies using

GRAPES simulations, Anderson et al. (1984) also model problem solving sessions in which the tutor presents a simplifying example to help repair incorrectly transferred LISP code. In both cases errors from inappropriate analogical inferences are repaired by introducing additional analogies. These must be integrated with the original analogy. In related psychological studies, Clement (1983) describes how expert problem solvers in physics use intermediate "bridging analogies" to help elaborate an analogical mapping between a target problem and a troublesome analogical source. *Each approach is computationally relevant and psychologically plausible, but integrating multiple analogies may introduce other difficulties. Multiple analogies, possibly at differing levels of abstraction, must be combined into a usable concept, avoiding what Halasz and Moran characterize as a "baroque collection of special-purpose models"* (1982, p. 34).

An integrated summary of the evaluative process component in analogical reasoning is given in the following passage (Hall 1989, 106, italics added):

In summary, analogical inferences must be treated, at best, as tentative hypotheses supported by a partial mapping between source and target domains. Domain interactions during evaluation confirm and repair analogical inferences extended during elaboration. Evaluation occurs at many levels: testing analogical predictions against expectations of what is typical of the target domain, verifying the utility of analogical inferences in some reasoning context, replaying justifications for analogical inferences in the target domain, and repairing inappropriate analogical inferences. *As a result of the evaluation process, parts of the analogical mapping may be changed or deleted, multiple analogies may be combined to suggest new hypotheses about the target domain, or the original analogy may be abandoned altogether in favor of an alternate line of reasoning.*

Process Component: Consolidation of the Analogy

The consolidation process component refers to the transfer of the verified knowledge contained in the analogy to subsequent problems, as described below (Hall 1989, 106, italics added):

The simplest form of consolidation directly records information successfully transferred from source to target domain. Of the reviewed studies that address consolidation, most perform this simple form of learning. For example, McDermott (1979) and Pirolli and Anderson (1985) record specific target productions; Hobbs (1983) creates and extends a target schema; Winston (1980, 1982) records successful target cases; and Greiner (1985) augments the starting theory with useful target conjectures. In each approach, learned material is strongly context-specific with little or no generalization. When facing a new task which is identical to an earlier success, the earlier solution is applied directly without resorting to more costly inference mechanisms. *Although this simple learning scheme might seem limited, when coupled with powerful recognition and elaboration processes, it could achieve incremental performance improvements as the collection of source candidates provides wider domain coverage.*

A number of computational systems store and reuse analogical content and reasoning, as described below (Hall 1989, 106–107):

For example, Winston (1978) stores transfer and justification frames. When reasoning about new similes, recognition first attempts to reuse an acquired transfer frame if related justification frames can be verified for the target. Using a similar approach, Pirolli and Anderson (1985) acquire task-specific mapping productions which supplant portions of later elaboration attempts. Other studies save the analogical mapping for the duration of an instructional context. For example, Brown (1977) and Burstein (1986) incrementally extend and repair a mapping as new tasks or feedback are given by a tutor. Although this may seem a matter of technical convenience, analogical reasoning is often an explicit component of tutorial interactions, and computational techniques of managing analogical comparisons (e.g., diagnosis or direct manipulation) can provide useful instructional or experimental tools.

To acquire knowledge with wider applicability, many studies form inductive summaries over target and source materials. Becker (1973), Winston (1982, 1986), and Pirolli and Anderson (1985) acquire generalized rules which consolidate inferences common to target and source. Becker's learner refines schemata through experience with a reactive environment; Winston's learner forms rules and censors from a series of predictive tasks presented by a tutor; and Pirolli's learner compiles analogical comparisons of declarative material into productions. Other studies use inductive mechanisms to form more complex plans or problem solving derivations common to target and source domains. For example, Carbonell (1983, 1986) consolidates successful transformational analogies into generalized solution sequences and derivational analogies into generalized plans and search heuristics. Similarly, Burstein (1986) argues for concept formation through analogies supported at varying levels of abstraction (e.g., causal inferences and plan steps) but includes learning from multiple analogical sources that cover different aspects of the target problem.

Analogical Reasoning: Problems and Solutions

Research problems and proposed solutions in the area of computational analogical reasoning are collated in Table 3.4

TABLE 3.4
Problems and Solutions across Components of
Analogical Reasoning

Recognition

Problem: Given a target and a store of *sources*, find a manageable but promising set of candidates.

Solutions: (1) Give the source as a simplification [Kling, 1971] or in a tutorial context [Burstein, 1986].

(2) Organize the store of sources around an indexing scheme:

    (a) nonselective indexing [Becker, 1973],

    (b) task-specific indexing [Winston, 1982],

    (c) task-independent indexing [Dyer, 1983a].

Elaboration

Problem: Given *target, source*, and mapping *preferences*, find a mapping and analogical inferences.

Solutions: (1) Use an existing analogy map [Winston, 1978].

(2) Prefer analogical mappings which:

    (a) preserve relational structure [Munyer, 1981],

    (b) preserve semantic categories [Simpson, 1985],

    (c) preserve contextual relevance [Kedar-Cabelli, 1985].

Evaluation

Problem: Given a mapping, analogical inferences, and a reasoning context, evaluate the analogy.

Solutions: (1) Confirm analogical inferences:

    (a) test predictions against target domain knowledge [Winston, 1978],

    (b) weigh the utility of inferences in context [Greiner, 1985],

    (c) replay a justification in the target domain (Carbonell, 1986].

(2) Repair faulty analogical inferences:

    (a) post failures as subgoals [McDermott, 1979],

    (b) integrate multiple analogies [Burstein, 1986].

(3) Monitor global progress:

    (a) heuristic thresholding [Munyer, 1981],

    (b) treat failure as a new problem [Simpson, 1985].

Consolidation

Problem: Given a *target, source*, and evaluated analogical inferences, consolidate these to improve future performance.

Solutions: (1) Record the target and outcome [McDermott, 1979].

(2) Record the analogical mapping [Winston, 1978].

(3) Record an inductive summary:

    (a) induce rules [Winston, 1986],

    (b) induce plan schema [Carbonell, 1983].

(4) Learn from failures:
   (a) record the failure to anticipate it later [McDermott, 1979],
   (b) record the failure remediation [Simpson, 1985],
   (c) refine analogy mechanisms [Carbonell, 1983].

Source: R. P. Hall, "Computational Approaches to Analogical Reasoning: A Comparative Analysis," *Artificial Intelligence* 39 (1989): 39–120. Reprinted with permission of Elsevier Science Publishers.

Process components of recognition, elaboration, evaluation and consolidation developed and discussed in preceding sections not only reflect the academic topography of work done in artificial intelligence and related disciplines, but these components also organize continuing research problems and proposed solutions. [Table 3.4] presents problems, proposed solutions, and citations to exemplary studies drawn from the comparative analysis of the preceding section.

Most work on analogical reasoning from a computational perspective addresses elaboration and evaluation, and alternative approaches to these problems can be clearly distinguished. Preferences for analogical mappings that preserve distinguished representational classes or contextually-relevant material constrain elaboration, while interactive constraints on confirmation, repair, and global monitoring of analogical inferences guide evaluation. As described in the preceding comparative analysis, these processes are strongly interdependent. In contrast, recognizing candidate analogs and consolidating information generated during their use have received less attention. However, differing approaches are also evident: alternative indexing schemes for organizing candidate sources constrain recognition, while a variety of analogically derived materials are learned during consolidation. Juxtaposed, these processes present a basic tension: recognizing analogies anticipates plausible inductive summarization, while consolidating confirmed analogical mappings attempts to predict future contexts of use.

Rather than solving basic problems in analogical reasoning, these approaches offer partial solutions, proposals, or refinements of larger problems. For example, replaying justifications for plan-level analogical inferences (Brown and Campione, 1985; Carbonell, 1986; and Kedar-Cabelli, 1985) refines the problem of elaboration and evaluating inferences at one level into a comparable problem at a lower level. For each analogy process component, the most ambitious and possibly most promising computational approaches have yet to be fully developed, implemented, or tested. Instead, implementations usually demonstrate carefully crafted solutions to isolated problems. Problems of scale and generality apply almost uniformly across the reviewed studies. This is less a criticism than an invitation to further analytical and empirical work. (Hall, 1989, 111–112)

Commentary

The abstract component process model of analogical reasoning is an important contribution to cognitive science. Its abstract character encompasses both human and artificial cognition; its componential structure enables differentiation and clarification of the global process of analogical reasoning. Although Hall (1989) concludes a review of computational and psychological studies on the note of "problems of scale and generality," two points need to be made. First, as new studies appear, the abstract component model can continue to deserve its systematizing function. Second, many more studies must be produced before integrated trends can be discerned.

4

Scientific Discovery

Scientific discovery processes involve a cyclical relationship between conjecture and experimentation. The discovery processes are complex and require sophisticated intellective abilities.

The development of scientific reasoning processes — including hypothesis, experiment, and their interaction — was investigated by D. Klahr, A. L. Fay, and K. Dunbar. Their interesting research will be described, and then a brief commentary will be presented.

SCIENTIFIC REASONING AND DEVELOPMENTAL DIFFERENCES

Overview

The following account summarizes the research of Klahr, Fay, and Dunbar (1993, 111):

Scientific discovery involves search in a space of hypotheses and a space of experiments. We describe an investigation of developmental differences in the search constraint heuristics used in scientific reasoning. Sixty-four subjects (technically trained college students, community college students with little technical training, sixth graders, and third graders) were taught how to use a programmable robot. Then they were presented with a new operation, provided with a hypothesis about how it might work, and asked to conduct experiments to discover how it really did work. The suggested hypothesis was always incorrect, as subjects could discover if they wrote informative experiments, and it was either plausible or implausible. The rule for how the unknown operation actually worked was either very similar or very dissimilar to the given hypothesis. Children focused primarily on plausible hypotheses, conducted a limited set of experiments, designed experiments that were difficult to interpret, and were unable to induce implausible (but correct) hypotheses from data. Adults were much better than children in discovering implausible rules. The performance deficits we found were not simply the result of children's inadequate encoding or mnemonic skills. Instead, the adults appear to use domain-general skills that go beyond the logic of confirmation and disconfirmation and deal with the coordination of search in two spaces: a space of hypotheses and a space of experiments.

Background

The following introduction to their research is provided by Klahr, Fay, and Dunbar (1993, 112–113, italics added):

Scientific discovery requires the integration of a complex set of cognitive skills, including the search for hypotheses via induction or analogy, the design and execution of experiments, the interpretation of experimental outcomes, and the revision of hypotheses (Klahr & Dunbar, 1988). There are two long-standing disputes about the developmental course of these skills: (a) the "child-as-scientist" debate asks whether or not it makes sense to describe the young child as a scientist; (b) the "domain-specific or domain-general" debate revolves around the appropriate attribution for whatever differences in children and adults may exist. The first issue is controversial because, although there is considerable evidence that young children possess some rudiments of scientific reasoning (Brewer & Samarapungavan, 1991; Karmiloff-Smith, 1988), there appears to be a long and erratic course of development, instruction, and experience before the component skills of the scientific method are mastered, integrated, and applied reliably to a wide range of situations (Fay, Klahr, & Dunbar, 1990; Kuhn, Amsel, & O'Loughlin, 1988; Mitroff, 1974; Kern, Mirels, & Hinshaw, 1983; Siegler & Liebert, 1975).

The second issue derives from a lack of consensus about the extent to which developmental differences in performance on scientific reasoning tasks results from domain-specific or domain-general acquisitions. . . . On the one hand, acquisition of domain-specific knowledge influences not only the substantive structural knowledge in the domain (by definition) but also the processes used to generate and evaluate new hypotheses in that domain (Carey, 1985; Keil, 1981; Wiser, 1989). On the other hand, in highly constrained discovery contexts, young children correctly reason about hypotheses and select appropriate experiments to evaluate them, even when the context is far removed from any domain-specific knowledge (Sodian, Zaitchik, & Carey, 1991).

The two principal ways (aside from direct instruction) in which children acquire such domain-specific knowledge are observation and experimentation. Analysis of children's performance as *observational* scientists is exemplified by Vosniadou and Brewer's (in press) investigations of children's mental models of the earth. Such studies involve assessments of children's attempts to integrate their personal observations (e.g., the earth looks flat) with theoretical assertions conveyed to them by adults and teachers (e.g., the earth is a sphere). Similarly, children's understanding of illness concepts (see Hergenrather & Rabinowitz, 1991) is based primarily on their observations in the domain, rather than on their experiments. Issues of experimental design do not arise in this context. *Experimental* science adds to the demands of observational science the burden of formulating informative experiments. Studies investigating young children's ability to design factorial experiments (Case, 1974; Siegler & Liebert, 1975) focus on experimental aspects of science, as do studies of children's performance in experimental microworlds (e.g., Schauble, 1990).

We have approached the study of developmental differences in scientific reasoning by attempting to disentangle these different aspects of scientific discovery, while using a context that provides a plausible laboratory microcosm of real-world scientific discovery. We view scientific discovery as a type of problem solving (Klahr & Dunbar, 1988; Simon, 1977) in which domain-general heuristics for constraining search in a problem space play a central role. *In this paper, we describe a study that illustrates some important developmental differences in subjects' use of several domain-general search heuristics. We compare the ability of children and adults to reason in a context designed to simulate some of the key problems faced by an experimental scientist. In our task, subjects' domain-specific knowledge biases them to view some hypotheses as plausible and others as implausible. However, they must rely on domain-general heuristics to guide them in designing experiments. In summary, our focus is on developmental differences in domain-general heuristics for experimental design, in a context where domain-specific knowledge influences the plausibility of different hypotheses.*

A theory of scientific discovery processes is presented in the following section (Klahr, Fay, & Dunbar 1993, 113–115, italics added):

We view scientific discovery as a problem-solving process involving search in two distinct, but related, problem spaces. Our work is based on Klahr and Dunbar's (1988) SDDS framework (Scientific Discovery as Dual Search), which elucidates a set of interdependent processes for coordinating search in a space of experiments and a space of hypotheses. The three main processes are:

1. *Searching the hypothesis space.* SDDS characterizes the process of generating new hypotheses as a type of problem-solving search, in which the initial state consists of some knowledge about a domain, and the goal state is a hypothesis that can account for some or all of that knowledge in a more concise or universal form. Several mechanisms have been proposed to account for the way in

which initial hypotheses are generated. These include memory search, analogical mapping, remindings, and discovery of effective representations (Dunbar & Schunn, 1990; Gentner, 1983; Gick & Holyoak, 1983; Kaplan & Simon, 1990; Klahr & Dunbar, 1988; Ross, 1984; Shrager, 1987). Each of these mechanisms emphasizes a different aspect of the way in which search in the hypothesis space is initiated and constrained.

Once generated, hypotheses are evaluated for their initial plausibility. Expertise plays a role here, as subjects' familiarity with a domain tends to give them strong biases about what is plausible in the domain. Plausibility, in turn, affects the order in which hypotheses are evaluated: highly likely hypotheses tend to be tested before unlikely hypotheses (Klayman & Ha, 1987; Wason, 1968). Furthermore, subjects may adopt different experimental strategies for evaluating plausible and implausible hypotheses.

2. *Searching the experiment space.* Hypotheses are evaluated through experimentation. But it is not immediately obvious what constitutes a "good" or "informative" experiment. In constructing experiments, subjects are faced with a problem-solving task paralleling their search for hypotheses. However, in this case search is in a space of experiments rather than in a space of hypotheses. Ideally, experiments should discriminate among rival hypotheses. Subjects must be able to plan ahead by making predictions about which experimental results could support or reject various hypotheses. This involves search in a space of experiments that is only partially defined at the outset. Constraints on the search must be added during the problem-solving process.

One of the most important constraints is to produce experiments that will yield interpretable outcomes. This, in turn, requires domain-general knowledge about one's own information-processing limitations, as well as domain-specific knowledge about the pragmatic constraints of the particular discovery context. Furthermore, utilization of this knowledge to design experiments capable of producing interpretable outcomes requires a mapping from hypotheses to experiments and an ability to predict what results might occur.

3. *Evaluating evidence.* This involves a comparison of the predictions derived from a hypothesis with the results obtained from the experiment. Compared to the binary feedback provided to subjects in the typical psychology experiment, real-world evidence evaluation is not so straightforward. Relevant features must first be extracted, potential noise must be suppressed or corrected, and the resulting internal representation must be compared with earlier predictions. Theoretical biases influence not only the strength with which hypotheses are held in the first place — and hence the amount of disconfirming evidence necessary to refute them — but also the features in the evidence that will be attended to and encoded (Wisniewski & Medin, 1991).

Each of the components listed above is a potential source of developmental change, and most investigators have studied them in isolation. . . . *We have approached the study of scientific reasoning by using tasks that require coordinated search in both the experiment space and the hypothesis space, as well as the evaluation of evidence produced by subject-generated experiments. Rather than eliminating search in either space, we have focused on the coordination of both, because we believe that it is an essential aspect of scientific reasoning.*

Design

Rationale

The rationale for the Klahr, Fay, and Dunbar research is summarized in the following account (1993, 115):

In this paper, we focus on developmental differences in the heuristics used to constrain search in the experiment space. We were interested in the extent to which such heuristics would vary according to age, amount of formal scientific training, and the plausibility of the hypotheses under investigation. Although most studies demonstrate that subjects tend to attempt to confirm, rather than disconfirm, their hypotheses (cf. Klayman & Ha, 1987), such studies typically use hypotheses about which subjects have no strong prior beliefs about plausibility or implausibility. In contrast, we used a context in which plausibility played an important role.

Results from earlier investigations (Dunbar & Klahr, 1989) suggested that, in the domain in which we planned to test them, subjects at all ages and technical levels would be likely to share *domain-specific* knowledge that would bias them in the same direction with respect to the relative plausibility of different hypotheses. This allowed us to determine how search in the experiment space was influenced by the hypothesis plausibility. We expected the effects of age and scientific training to reveal differences in the *domain-general* heuristics used to constrain search in the experiment space. Such domain-general heuristics might include rules for effecting normative approaches to hypothesis testing as well as pragmatic rules for dealing with processing limitations in encoding, interpreting, and remembering experimental outcomes.

Subjects

Research subjects are described in the following section (Klahr, Fay, & Dunbar 1993, 115–116):

Four subject groups participated: 12 Carnegie Mellon (CM) undergraduates, 20 community college (CC) students, 17 "sixth" graders (a mixed class of fifth to seventh graders, mean age 11 years) and 15 third graders (mean age, 9 years). The adult groups were selected to contrast subjects with respect to technical and scientific training. Sixth graders were selected because they represent the age at which many of the components of "formal reasoning" are purported to be available, and the third graders were chosen because pilot work had indicated they were the youngest group who could perform reliably in our task. In addition, the two younger groups match the ages of children studied in many other investigations of children's scientific reasoning skills (e.g., Kuhn et al., 1988).

CMs were mainly science or engineering majors. . . . They reported having taken about two programming courses, and they rated themselves between average and above average on technical and scientific skills. All CCs were nonscience majors (General Studies, Paralegal, Communications, Pre-nursing, etc.). . . . CCs had little training in mathematics or physical sciences beyond high school, and less than half of them had taken a college course in Biology or Chemistry. While 70% of them had used computer-based word processors and 45% had used spreadsheets, only 3 of the 20 had ever taken a programming course.

Children were volunteers from an urban private school and came primarily from academic and professional families. They were selected to be young "equivalents" of the CMs with respect to both the likelihood of ultimately attending college and age-appropriate computer experience. All sixth graders had at least 6 months of Logo experience, and most had more than a year of experience. All but one of the third graders had at least 1 month of Logo, with the majority having 6 months to a year of experience. Note that CCs had less programming experience than the third graders.

Material: The BT Microworld

Experiment material is described in the following section (Klahr, Fay, & Dunbar 1993, 116):

We used a computer microworld — called BT — in which subjects enter a sequence of commands to a "spaceship" which then responds by carrying out various maneuvers. The discovery context was established by first instructing subjects about all of BT's basic features and then asking them to extend that knowledge by discovering how a new — and uninstructed — function works in the microworld. Subjects proposed hypotheses and evaluated them by experimenting, i.e., by writing programs to test their hypotheses.

The spaceship moves around in the left-hand panel according to instructions that are entered in its memory when subjects "press" (point and click) a sequence of keys on the keypad displayed on the right. The basic execution cycle involves first clearing the memory and returning BT to "base" with the CLR/HOME key and then entering a series of up to 16 instructions, each consisting of a function key (the command) and a 1- or 2-digit number (the argument). The five command keys are: ↑, move forward; ↓, move backward; ←, turn left; →, turn right; and FIRE. When the GO key is pressed BT executes the program. For example, one might press the following series of keys:

CLR ↑ 5 ← 7 ↑ 3 → 15 FIRE 2 ↓ 8 GO

When the GO key was pressed, BT would move forward 5 units, rotate coun-
terclockwise 42° (corresponding to 7 min on an ordinary clock face), move forward 3 units, rotate clockwise 90°, fire (its "laser cannon") twice, and backup 8
units.

Experimental Procedure

Details of the experimental procedure are provided in the following
paragraphs (Klahr, Fay, & Dunbar 1993, 116–117):

The study had three phases. In the first, subjects were introduced to BT and
instructed on the use of each basic command. During this phase, the display did
not include the RPT key. . . . Subjects were trained to criterion on how to write a
series of commands to accomplish a specified maneuver. In the second phase,
subjects were shown the RPT key. They were told that it required a numeric para-
meter (N) and that there could only be one RPT N in a program. They were told
that their task was to find out how RPT worked by writing at least three programs
and observing the results. At this point, the Experimenter suggested a specific
hypothesis about how RPT might work.

One way that RPT might work is: [one of the four hypotheses described in the
next section]. Write down three good programs that will allow you to see if the
repeat key really does work this way. Think carefully about your program and
then write the program down on the sheet of paper. . . . Once you have written your program down, I will type it in for you and then I will run it. You can
observe what happens, and then you can write down your next program. So
you write down a program, then I will type it in, and then you will watch what
the program does. I want you to write three programs in this way.

Next, the third — and focal — phase began. Subjects wrote programs (experiments) to evaluate the given hypothesis. After each program had been written,
but before it was run, subjects were asked to predict the behavior of BT. Subjects
had access to a record of the programs they had written (but not to a record of
BT's behavior).

Subjects were instructed to give verbal protocols. This gave us a record of (a)
what they thought about the kinds of programs they were writing while testing
their hypotheses, (b) what they observed and inferred from the device's behavior,
and (c) what their hypotheses were about how RPT actually worked. When subjects had written, run, and evaluated three experiments, they were given the
option of either terminating or writing additional experiments if they were still
uncertain about how RPT worked. The entire session lasted approximately 45
min.

Experimental Task Analysis: The Hypothesis Space

An analysis of the experimental hypothesis space is presented in the following account (Klahr, Fay, & Dunbar 1993, 118–119):

In previous studies with adults and grade school children (Klahr & Dunbar, 1988), we found that there were two very "popular" hypotheses about the effect of RPT N in a program:

A: Repeat the entire program *N* times.
B: Repeat the last step *N* times.

Subjects devoted a large proportion of their efforts to exploring these two hypotheses. In contrast, there were two hypotheses that subjects were unlikely to propose at the outset:

C: Repeat the *N*th step once.
D: Repeat the last *N* steps once.

The preference for A and B and the disinclination to propose C and D were found at all ages.

These four hypotheses about RPT N (as well as many others) can be represented in a space of "frames" (Minsky, 1975). The basic frame consists of four slots, corresponding to four key attributes: (1) the role of N; does it *count* a number of repetitions (as in A and B) or does it *select* some segment of the program to be repeated (as in C and D)? We call A and B *Counter* hypotheses and C and D *Selector* hypotheses. (2) The unit of repetition; is it a step (as in B and C), the entire program (as in A), or a group of steps (as in D)? (3) Number of repetitions; 1, *N*, some other function of *N*, or none? (4) Boundaries of repeated segment; beginning of program, end of program, *N*th step from beginning, or end? Of the four slots, *N*-role is the most important, because a change in *N*-role from *Counter* to *Selector* mandates a change in several other attributes. For example, if *N*-role is *Counter*, the number of repetitions is *N*, whereas, if *N*-role is *Selector*, then the number of repetitions is 1.

Experimental Task Analysis: The Experiment Space

An analysis of the experiment space is provided in the following section (Klahr, Fay, & Dunbar 1993, 118–119):

Subjects could test their hypotheses by conducting experiments, i.e., by writing programs that included RPT and observing BT's behavior. The BT experiment space can be characterized in many ways: the total number of commands in a program, the location of RPT in a program, value of *N*, the specific commands in a program, the numerical arguments of specific commands, and so on. (For example, counting only commands, but not their numerical arguments, as distinct, there are over 30 billion distinct programs [5^{15}] that subjects could choose from for each experiment. Even if we consider only programs with 4 or fewer steps, there are nearly 800 different experiments to choose from [$5^4 + 5^3 + 5^2 + 5$].) In this paper, we characterize the experiment space in terms of just two parameters. The first is λ — the length of the program preceding the RPT. The second is the value of N — the argument that RPT takes. Because both parameters must have values less than 16, there are 225 "cells" in the λ–N space. Within that space, we identify three distinct regions. Region 1 includes all programs with $N = 1$. Region 2 includes all programs in which $1 < N < \lambda$. Region 3 includes all programs in which $N \geq \lambda$. The regions are depicted in [Figure 4.1] together with illustrative programs, from the (4,1) cell in Region 1, the (3,2) cell in Region 2, and the (1,4) cell in Region 3.

Programs from different regions of the experiment space vary widely in how effective they are in supporting or refuting different hypotheses. (A complete analysis of the interaction between experiment space regions and hypotheses is given in Klahr, Dunbar, & Fay (1990). Here we summarize the major differences between the regions.)

1. Region 1 programs have poor discriminating power. For example, the Region 1 program shown in [Figure 4.1] would execute the final LT 5 command twice under both Rule B (Repeat the last step N times) and Rule D (Repeat the last N steps once).
2. Region 2 programs provide maximal information about all of the common hypotheses, because they can distinguish between Counters and Selectors, and they can distinguish *which* Selector or Counter is operative. Region 2 produces different behavior under all four rules for any program in the region, and varying N in a series of experiments in this region always produces different outcomes.
3. Region 3 experiments may yield confusing outcomes. For rules C (Repeat the Nth step once) and D (Repeat the last N steps once), programs in this region are executed under the subtle feature that values of N greater than λ are truncated to $N = \lambda$. Therefore, varying N from one experiment to the next may give the impression that N has no effect. For example, Rule D would generate the same behavior for ↑ 4 Fire 2 RPT 3 and ↑ 4 Fire 2 RPT 4. Some of the programs in this region are discriminating, but others either don't discriminate at all, or they depend on the truncation assumption to be fully understood.

Experimental Controls

Details of the experimental conditions are provided in the following section (Klahr, Fay, & Dunbar 1993, 119–120, italics added):

One consequence of domain-specific knowledge is that some hypotheses about the domain are more plausible than others. In this study we explored the effect of

FIGURE 4.1

Regions of the Experiment Space, Showing Illustrative Programs

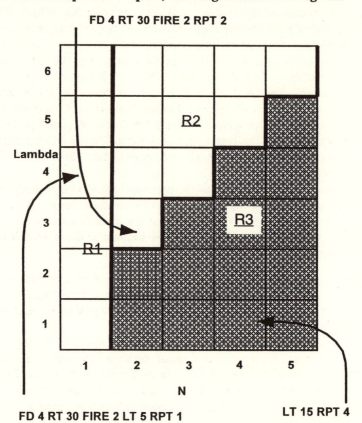

Note: Shown here is only the 6 x 5 subspace of the full 15 x 15 space.

Source: D. Klahr, A. L. Fay, and K. Dunbar, "Heuristics for Scientific Experimentation: A Developmental Study," *Cognitive Psychology* 25 (1993): 111–146. Reprinted with permission of Academic Press.

domain-specific knowledge by manipulating the role of plausible and implausible hypotheses. Our goal was to investigate the extent to which prior knowledge — as manifested in hypothesis plausibility — affected the types of experiments designed and the interpretation of results.

We provided each subject with an initial hypothesis about how RPT might work. The suggested hypothesis was always wrong. However, depending on the condition, subjects regarded it as either plausible or implausible (recall that both children and adults in earlier studies regarded Counter hypotheses as highly plausible and Selector hypotheses as implausible). In some conditions the suggested hypothesis was only "somewhat" wrong, in that it was from the same frame as the way that RPT actually worked. In others, it was "very" wrong, in that it came from a different frame than the actual rule.

The BT simulator was programmed so that each subject worked with a RPT command obeying one of the two Counter rules or two Selector rules described above. We used a between-subjects design, depicted in [Table 4.1]. The Given hypothesis is the one that was suggested by the experimenter, and the Actual Rule is the way that BT was programmed to work for a particular condition. The key feature is that RPT *never worked in the way that was suggested.* In each Given-Actual condition, there were three CMs, five CCs, four sixth graders, and four third graders (except for the Counter-Counter condition, which had three third graders and five sixth graders).

Changing from a hypothesis within a frame to another hypothesis from the same frame (e.g., from one Counter to another Counter) corresponds to theory refinement. However, as noted earlier, a change in N-role requires a simultaneous change in more than one attribute, because the values of some attributes are linked to the values of others. *Changing from a hypothesis from one frame to a hypothesis from a different frame (e.g., from a Counter to a Selector) corresponds to theory replacement.*

Experimental Protocols

General aspects of subject protocols are described, and a specific subject protocol is provided in the following section (Klahr, Fay, & Dunbar 1993, 120–121, italics added):

The raw protocols provided the basis for all performance measures. They are comprised of subjects' written programs as well as transcriptions of subjects' verbalizations during the experimental phase. Before presenting the quantitative analysis of subjects' behavior, we examine the verbal protocol of a single subject in order to illustrate a variety of interesting qualitative aspects of subjects' behavior. . . . Our goal is to convey a general sense of subjects' approach to the task and to illustrate how we encoded and interpreted the protocols. In subsequent sections, we provide a detailed analysis based on the full set of protocols.

DP was a male CM subject in the Counter-Selector condition, and he was given Rule A: *Repeat entire program N times.* The actual rule was Rule C: *Repeat Nth step once.* DP discovered the correct rule after five experiments. Two characteristics of DP's protocol make it interesting (but not atypical). First, even before the first experiment, DP proposed an alternative to the Given hypothesis (2: "I want to test to see if RPT repeats the statements before it"). Second, throughout the experimental phase, DP made many explicit comments about the attributes of the experiment space. He clearly attended to the properties of a "good" experiment.

TABLE 4.1
Design of Given-Actual Conditions

		Actual Rule	
Given Hypothesis	**Counter**	**Counter**	**Selector**
Counter		B: Repeat last step N times → A: Repeat entire program N times	A: Repeat entire program N times → D: Repeat the last N steps once
Selector		D: Repeat the last N steps once → A: Repeat the entire program N times	C: Repeat step N once → D: Repeat the last N steps once

Source: D. Klahr, A. L. Fay, and K. Dunbar, "Heuristics for Scientific Experimentation: A Developmental Study," *Cognitive Psychology* 25 (1993): 111–146. Reprinted with permission of Academic Press.

DP's goal in his first experiment is unambiguous (2-9): to determine whether RPT acts on instructions before or after the RPT command. To resolve this question DP concluded an experiment with easily distinguished commands before and after the RPT key. (This ability to write programs that contain useful "markers" is an important feature of our subjects' behavior, and we will return to it later.) This experiment allowed DP to discriminate between these two rival hypotheses. However, with respect to discriminating between the Given hypothesis (A), the Current hypothesis (B) and the Actual hypothesis (C), the program yielded ambiguous results. DP extracted from the first experiment the information he sought (17–18: "it appears that the repeat doesn't have any effect on any statements that come after it").

For the second experiment DP returned to the question of whether the Given hypothesis (A), or the Current hypothesis (B) was correct, and he increased λ from 1 to 2. He also included one step following the RPT "just to check" that RPT had no effect on instructions that follow it (22–23). Thus, DP was in fact testing three hypotheses; A, B, and "after." Once again, he used commands that could be easily discriminated. He wrote another program from Region 3 of the experiment space ($\lambda = 2$, $N = 2$). DP observed that there were two executions of the ↑ 2 instruction, and he concluded (29–30) that "it only repeats the statement immediately in front of it." While this conclusion is consistent with the data that DP had collected so far, the hypothesis (B) was not in fact how the RPT key worked.

For the third experiment, DP continued to put commands after RPT just to be sure they were not affected. However, given that his current hypothesis had been confirmed in the previous experiment, he next wrote a program that further increased the length of the program. This was his first experiment in Region 2. The goal of this experiment was to "see what statements are repeated" (33). He realized that the outcome of this experiment was inconsistent with his Current hypothesis (B), while the outcome of the previous experiment was consistent with B (47: ". . . it seemed to act differently in number two and number three"). The unexpected result led DP to abandon Hypothesis B and to continue beyond the mandatory three experiments.

For the fourth experiment, DP used a different value of N (53–54: ". . . repeat three instead of repeat two, and see if that has anything to do with it"). Here too, DP demonstrated another important characteristic of many of our subjects' approaches to experimentation. He used a very conservative incremental strategy, similar to VOTAT (vary one thing at a time) strategies described by Tschirgi (1980) and the Conservative Focusing strategy described by Bruner, Goodnow, and Austin (1956). This approach still led him to put commands after the RPT, even though he was confident that RPT had no effect on them, and even though they placed greater demands on his observational and recall processes. (At the $\lambda - N$ level, DP executed VOTAT consistently throughout his series of five experiments. The $\lambda - N$ pairs were: 1–2, 2–2, 3–2, 3–3, 3–1. For the last three experiments, even the specific commands and their parameters remained the same, and only N varied.) This moved him from Region 2 into Region 3, and while analyzing the results of this experiment (59–69) in conjunction with earlier results, DP changed from the Counter frame to the Selector frame. First he noticed that "the number three" statement (i.e., the ↓ 1) was repeated twice in this case but that "the turning statement" was repeated (i.e., executed) only once (59–61). The implied comparison was with the previous experiment in which the turning statement (i.e., "the right 15 command" [43]) was the command that got repeated.

The next sentence is of particular interest: ". . . because when I change the number not only did it change . . . it didn't change the uh . . . the number that it repeated but it changed the uh . . . the actual instruction" (64–67). We believe that DP was attempting to articulate a change from the Counter frame to the Selector frame, as the following paraphrase of his comments indicates: "When I changed the value of N, it didn't change the number of repetitions, but it did change which commands got repeated."

DP went on to clearly state two instantiated versions of the correct rule by referring to previous results with N = 2 and N = 3, and he designed his fifth experiment to test his prediction with N = 1. The outcome of this final experiment, from Region 1, in conjunction with earlier results was sufficient to convince him that he had discovered how RPT worked.

Results

Differential Success Rates

Findings concerning success rates are presented in the following section (Klahr, Fay, & Dunbar 1993, 122):

Domain-specific knowledge — as manifested in subjects' expectations about what "repeat" might mean in this context — played an important role in subjects' ability to discover the Actual rule. . . . Regardless of what the Given hypothesis was, subjects found it easier to discover Counters (81%) than Selectors (35%). . . . There was also a main effect for group: the correct rule was discovered by 83% of the CMs, 65% of the CCs, 53% of the sixth graders, and 33% of the third graders. . . . This group effect is attributable to the Actual = Selector conditions, in which 56% of the adults but only 13% of the children were successful. . . . For Counters, adults and children were roughly equal in their success rates (88% versus 75%).

The main effect for plausibility can also be attributed primarily to the children's performance in the Actual = Selector condition. Whereas 75% of the children discovered the rule when it was a Counter, only 13% discovered the rule when it was a Selector. . . . Adults were also better at discovering Counters than Selectors (88% versus 56%), although the effect was not as strong as for children

. . . due to the surprisingly poor performance by the CC subjects in the Counter-Counter condition.

Hypothesis Interpretation and Search

Findings concerning the effect of hypothesis plausibility on search behavior are presented in the following section (Klahr, Fay, & Dunbar 1993, 123–125, italics added):

The purpose of presenting subjects with a Given hypothesis was to determine the extent to which search in the hypothesis space was influenced by the plausibility of the hypothesis being considered. This is one of the points at which domain-specific knowledge (which determines plausibility) might affect domain-general knowledge about experimental strategies, such as attempts to disconfirm, discriminating between rival hypotheses, and so on.

Prior to running the first experiment, subjects were asked to predict what would happen. Their predictions indicated the extent to which they understood and/or accepted the Given hypotheses. Each subject's response to the Given hypothesis was assigned to one of three categories: I, accept the Given hypothesis; II, accept the Given, but also propose an alternative (see the protocol of Subject DP, presented earlier); and III, reject the Given, and propose an alternative.

There was a main effect of Given hypothesis (Counter versus Selector) on type of response. . . . This effect was attributable entirely to the third graders, who almost always accepted Counters and rejected Selectors. . . . There was also a main effect for group.

In both conditions, the two adult groups always accepted the Given hypothesis, either on its own (Category I) or in conjunction with a proposed alternative (Category II). . . . In contrast, no third grader and only two sixth graders ever proposed an alternative to compare to the Given (Category II). Children were approximately evenly divided between accepting the Given (Category I) or rejecting it (Category III). . . . Overall, adults were more likely to consider multiple alternatives than children: 10 of 29 adults in Category II, versus 2 of 31 children.

Of the 25 subjects who proposed alternatives to the Given hypothesis, three proposed alternatives that could not be coded as either Counters or Selectors. For the remaining 22, there was a strong effect of the type of Given hypothesis on the type of alternative proposed. . . . In each group, Given = Counter subjects who proposed alternatives always proposed another Counter, whereas, across all four groups, only two of the Given = Selector alternatives were from the Selector frame.

In summary, when responding to the Given hypothesis, adults were able to consider more than a single hypothesis, whereas children were not. When subjects did propose alternatives, they tended to propose plausible rather than implausible alternatives (i.e., Counters rather than Selectors). As we shall see in the next section, this propensity to consider multiple versus single hypotheses can affect the type of experimental goals set by the subjects, which in turn can be used to impose constraints on search in the experiment space.

Experiment Space Search

Experiment search strategies are described in the following section (Klahr, Fay, & Dunbar 1993, 129):

Different experimental strategies can . . . be inferred by classifying experiments in terms of experiment space regions. . . . As noted earlier, Region 2 is the most informative region, and adults appear to have understood its potential informativeness better than the children. Eleven of 12 CMs, 15 of 20 CCs, 10 of 17 sixth graders, and 8 of 15 third graders wrote at least one Region 2 experiment. . . . Another way to extract useful information from the E-space is to write experiments from more than a single region. Adults were more likely to sample different regions than were children. Ninety-one percent of the adults (100% of the CMs and 85% of the CCs) wrote experiments from at least two different regions of the experiment space. In contrast, only 29% of the sixth graders and 6% of the third graders sampled from more than one region. . . . Staying in one region of the experiment space is only detrimental if the region fails to discriminate between hypotheses (e.g., Region 1 for hypotheses B versus D) or if it fails to adequately demonstrate the correct hypothesis (e.g., Region 3 for hypothesis D). All of the third graders in Actual = Selector conditions who stayed in one region were in either Region 1 or 3. For the sixth graders in Actual = Selector conditions, 75% who stayed in one region were in Region 3. Thus, for the children, the failure to run experiments from different regions of the experiment space severely limited their ability to extract useful information from the outcomes of their experiments.

The common pattern here is that there is little or no difference between the CM and CC subjects, who, when combined, tend to differ from the two children's groups. For some measures, the sixth graders cluster with the adult subjects. Taken as a whole, this pattern suggests a developmental effect, rather than a training effect, for subjects' sensitivity to the potential informativeness of different types of experiments as a function of the Given hypothesis. Moreover, by some of our measures, this effect appears between third and sixth grades.

Relating Experiment Outcomes to Hypotheses

Subjects' ability to coordinate experiment outcomes and hypothesis modification are analyzed in the following section (Klahr, Fay, & Dunbar 1993, 132–133):

In order to determine the effect of experiment space region on overall success rate, we calculated the probability of discovering the correct rule as a function of the Regions actually visited. When success rates are aggregated over all grades and conditions, there appears to be no benefit from having been in Region 2. Sixty-four percent of the 44 subjects who had one or more Region 2 experiments were successful, while 45% of the 20 who never entered Region 2 were successful. . . . However, as predicted, a closer analysis reveals a clear effect of Region 2's utility for discovering Selectors. . . . As just noted, most subjects in the Actual = Counter conditions were successful, regardless of whether or not they entered Region 2. However, for all but one subject in the Actual = Selector conditions, having at least one experiment in Region 2 is a necessary but not sufficient condition for success.

DISCUSSION OF SCIENTIFIC DISCOVERY HEURISTICS AND DEVELOPMENTAL DIFFERENCES

Heuristics for Experiment Space Search

Differences and similarities in subjects' use of heuristics to search in the experiment space are discussed in the following section (Klahr, Fay, & Dunbar 1993, 134–136):

Both CM and CC adults were effective at drastically pruning the experiment space. Over half of their experiments occurred within the $\lambda \leq 4$, $N \leq 3$ area of the experiment space, which represents only 5% of the full space. In contrast, less than one-third of the children's experiments were so constrained. Furthermore, the pattern of results described in the previous section revealed a developmental trend in the overall systematicity and effectiveness with which subjects searched the experiment space. Our interpretation of this pattern is that it is a consequence of developmental differences in the application of a set of domain-general heuristics for searching the experiment space. The four principle heuristics are:

1. *Use the plausibility of a hypothesis to choose experimental strategy.* . . . For implausible hypotheses, adults and young children used different strategies. Adults' response to implausibility was to propose hypotheses from frames other than the Given frame and to conduct experiments that could discriminate between them. Our youngest children's response was to propose a hypothesis from a different, but plausible frame, and then to ignore the initial, and implausible, hypothesis while attempting to demonstrate the correctness of the plausible one. Third graders were particularly susceptible to this strategy, but by sixth grade, subjects appeared to understand the type of experiments that will be informative.

2. *Focus on one dimension of an experiment or hypothesis.* Experiments and hypotheses are both complex entities having many aspects on which one could focus. In this study, experiments could vary at the $\lambda - N$ level, at the command level, or even at the level of arguments for commands.

Use of this focusing heuristic was manifested in different ways with respect to hypotheses and experiments. For hypotheses, it led all groups except the third graders to focus initially on the number of times something was repeated when given Counters, and what was repeated when given Selectors. . . . For experiments, it led to a characteristic pattern of between-experiment moves that minimized changes at the command level. Here, the CM adults stood apart from the other three groups. They were much more likely than any of the three groups to make conservative moves — that is, to minimize differences in program content between one program and the next. Although there are few sequential dependencies in the informativeness of experiment space regions, CM adults may have used this heuristic to reduce the cognitive load imposed when comparing the outcomes of two programs.

Interestingly, only the third graders failed to use this heuristic when searching the hypothesis space, whereas only the CM adults used it effectively when searching the experiment space. It is possible that, because the hypothesis search aspect of the discovery task is so familiar, all but the third graders were able to use the focusing heuristic. In contrast, when confronted with the relatively novel experimental design aspect of the task, even adults, if untrained in science, remained unaware of the utility of a conservative change strategy.

3. *Maintain observability.* As BT moves along the screen from one location to another, it leaves no permanent record of its behavior. Subjects must remember what BT actually did. Thus, one heuristic is to write short programs in order to make it easy to remember what happened and to compare the results to those predicted by the Current hypotheses. At the level of individual commands, this heuristic produces small arguments for the ↑ and ↓ commands, so that BT does not go off the screen. There were clear differences in the use of this heuristic. Adults almost always used it, whereas the youngest children often wrote programs that were very difficult to encode. This heuristic depends upon knowledge of one's own information processing limitations as well as a knowledge of the device.

4. *Design experiments giving characteristic results.* Physicians look for "markers" for diseases, and physicists design experiments in which suspected particles will leave "signatures." In the BT domain, this heuristic is instantiated as "use many distinct commands." This heuristic maximizes the interpretability of experimental outcomes. It is extremely difficult to isolate the cause of a particular piece of BT behavior when many of the commands in a program are the same. All four groups were roughly equivalent in their use of this heuristic; on average, about half of all programs did not contain any repeated commands.

Overall, adults and children differed widely in their use of these heuristics. Adults not only appeared to use each of them but also appeared to be able to deal with their inherent contradictions. No subject ever used the 1,1 cell, even though it would yield the easiest to observe behavior, because it is so uninformative with respect to discriminating among rival hypotheses. Additionally, in a related study (Klahr, Dunbar, & Fay, 1990), adults' experiments were significantly *over*represented in the $\lambda = 3$, $N = 2$ cell of the experiment space. This cell represents the shortest possible Region 2 experiment, and its overrepresentation suggests a compromise between informativeness and simplicity. Adults' tendency to cluster their experiments in the 4 x 3 experiment space in the present study represents a similar compromise among competing heuristics.

In contrast, children either failed to use these heuristics at all or they let one of them dominate. For example, one approximation to the "characteristic result" heuristic would be to write long experiments that could generate unique behavior, although that would violate the "maintain observability" heuristic. Even on their first experiments, adults tended to write relatively short programs. Only one-third of them wrote first programs with $\lambda > 3$, whereas 80% of the children wrote programs with $\lambda > 3$.

Developmental Differences in Scientific Problem Solving

The scientific reasoning behavior of adults and children is compared in the following section (Klahr, Fay, & Dunbar 1993, 139–141, italics added):

Our study yielded a picture of both similarities and differences in the way that children and adults formulate hypotheses and design experiments to evaluate them. At the top level of the cycle of scientific reasoning — that is, the level of hypothesis formation, experimentation and outcome interpretation — older elementary school children approached the discovery task in an appropriate way. Most sixth graders and some third graders understood that their task was to produce evidence to be used in support of an argument about a hypothesis. Contrary to Kuhn et al. (1988), they were able to distinguish between theory (hypotheses) and evidence. However, when placed in a context requiring the coordination of search in two spaces, children's performances were markedly inferior to adults (both with and without technical and scientific training).

An examination of the fine structure of the subjects' sequences of experiments and hypotheses revealed that their overall performance differences could be attributed to characteristic differences in how they searched both the hypothesis space and the experiment space. The most important difference in hypothesis space search was in the way that adults and children responded to plausible and implausible hypotheses. When adults were given an implausible hypothesis, they established a goal of designing an experiment that could discriminate between the given implausible hypothesis and a plausible hypothesis of their own creation (usually one of the standard Counters).

When children were given hypotheses to evaluate, they were not insensitive to whether they were plausible or implausible, but they responded by generating a different goal than the adults. In the implausible case, rather than simultaneously considering two alternative hypotheses, children focused only on a plausible one of their own making (a Counter), and attempted to generate what they believed would be extremely convincing evidence for it. This was not an unreasonable goal, but it produced uninformative experiments. More specifically, in order to generate a convincing case for a Counter hypothesis, third graders chose large values of N, so that the effect of the number of repetitions would be unambiguous. Because their goal was demonstration, inconsistencies were interpreted not as disconfirmations, but rather as either errors or temporary failures to demonstrate the desired effect. When subsequent efforts to demonstrate the Counter hypothesis were successful, they were accepted as sufficient. Because the third graders did not seek global consistency, they extracted only local information from experimental outcomes. Analogous results with respect to lack of global consistency have been reported by Markman (1979). She demonstrated that children between 8 and 11 years old have difficulty noticing internal contradictions in relatively brief text passages. Markman suggested that children focus on the reasonableness of individual statements, rather than their collective consistency. Similarly, our youngest children selectively focused on specific experimental outcomes, rather than seeking a hypothesis that could account for all of them.

The BT context elicited behavior in our third graders that is characteristic of younger children in simpler contexts. Resistance to disconfirming evidence has been observed in studies of discrimination learning (Tumblin & Gholson, 1981), but it has been limited to much younger children. For example, Gholson, Levine, and Phillips (1972) found that kindergarten children maintained disconfirmed hypotheses on about half of the negative feedback trials, while by second grade the rate dropped to 10%. The complexity of the discovery context, in conjunction with strong plausibility biases, may have caused our third graders to function like kindergarten children in the simpler discrimination learning task.

With respect to search heuristics in the experiment space, children were less able than adults to constrain their search, they tended not to consider pragmatic constraints, and they were unsystematic in the way that they designed experiments. These findings indicate that one of the problems for the younger children is to apply effective search constraints on their experiments. This viewpoint is consistent with research on the effects of constraints on problem solving in younger children. When presented with "standard" puzzles (involving search in a single problem space), young children perform much better when the order of subgoals is constrained by the structure of the materials than when they have to decide for themselves what to do first (Klahr, 1985; Klahr & Robinson, 1981). Here too, we find the third graders in our dual-search situation behaving analogously to younger children in single-search contexts. That is, in our study, when given a task in which they had to impose multiple constraints on hypotheses and experimental design, children did not conduct appropriate experiments. However, in studies where both hypotheses and experimental choices are highly constrained, young children can select appropriate experiments (Sodian et al., 1991).

Overall, the SDDS framework has helped us to begin to answer some enduring questions about the development of scientific discovery skills. The results of our analysis, when combined with the related work from other laboratories, clarify the conditions under which children's domain-general reasoning skills are adequate to successfully coordinate search for hypotheses and experiments: (a) hypotheses must be easily accessible (such as the highly plausible Counters in our study) or few in number (as in the two-alternative situations used by Sodian et al.), (b) the experimental alternatives must also be few in number (also as in Sodian et al.), and (c) the domain must provide feedback relevant to discriminating among plausible hypotheses (as in Region 2 experiments in BT studies). It is important to reiterate the point that the performance deficits we found were not simply the result of children's inadequate encoding or mnemonic skills. As shown earlier, when experimental outcomes were consistent with children's expectations, they were correctly encoded, even though they were three times as long as those incorrectly encoded, but discrepant from children's expectations. Instead, the adult superiority appears to come from a set of domain-general skills that go beyond the logic of confirmation and disconfirmation and deal with the coordination of search in two spaces.

Commentary

Beyond examining the interesting specific results of experimental research, it is important to inquire into generalizations that can be drawn.

Scientific and technical training facilitated success in the experimental task. The central heuristic of varying one item at a time is an efficient problem-solving strategy acquired during formal university training in scientific laboratory procedures.

The conceptual account of scientific discovery as the coordination of search in hypothesis and experiment spaces is a highly valuable contribution to the philosophy of science. The validity of scientific explanation depends on the establishment of coherence between hypothesis and evidence, and the competence of scientific prediction depends on the establishment of correspondence between experimental expectation and experimental outcome. Discovery, explanation, and prediction all require the interpenetration of knowledge in the space of hypotheses and the space of experiments.

5

Language

ARTIFICIAL INTELLIGENCE AND THE PRAGMATICS OF LANGUAGE GENERATION

> It never happens that [the automaton] arranges its speech in various ways, in order to reply appropriately to everything that may be said in its presence, as even the lowest type of man can do.
> — Descartes, quoted in Wilson 1969, 138

"Explanations by human experts, in general, are tailored to their audiences. The details of reasoning as related to another expert in the same domain will be different from those related to a layman. This requires a kind of intelligent behavior not apparent in the explanation facilities of current expert systems" (Hayes-Roth, Waterman, & Lenat 1983, 49).

The problem of how to inculcate flexibility in a language generation program so as to take account of pragmatics — that is, the intentionality intended by the speaker and interpreted by the hearer — was investigated by L. H. Hovy. In this section, the general logic, principles, features, behavioral examples, and limitations of the computer language generation program PAULINE (Planning And Uttering Language In Natural Environments) (Hovy 1990) will be described; then, in a commentary section, general issues of artificial intelligence approaches to the pragmatics of language generation will be examined.

PAULINE

General Logic

Two general principles govern the development of PAULINE: the principle of rhetorical strategies and the principle of interweaving generation processes. Beyond the rules themselves, it is important to note that these two general principles are inclusive of computers and humans. Furthermore, although any one program such as PAULINE may be confined to a given topic in its elaborative details, the general rules hold and guide the program's development and execution. Hovy's general research questions are summarized in the following section (1990, 153):

This paper addresses the question "why and how is it that we say the same thing differently to different people, or even to the same person in different circumstances?" We vary the content and form of our text in order to convey more information than is contained in the literal meanings of our words. This information expresses the speaker's interpersonal goals toward the hearer and, in general, his or her perception of the pragmatic aspects of the conversation. This paper discusses two insights that arise when one studies this question: the existence of a level of organization that mediates between communicative goals and generator decisions, and the interleaved planning-realization regime and associated monitoring required for generation. To illustrate these ideas, a computer program is described which contains plans and strategies to produce stylistically appropriate texts from a single representation under various settings that model pragmatic circumstances.

The theoretical assumptions underlying the development of PAULINE are presented in the following account (Hovy 1990, 155–156; italics added):

In order for generator programs to produce similarly varied, information-bearing text, such programs must have some means of representing relevant characteristics of the hearer, the conversation setting, and their interpersonal goals. These are the *pragmatic* concerns. In addition, they must contain choice points in the grammar that enable topics to be said in various ways. These are the *syntactic* concerns. Finally, they require criteria by which to make the decisions so that the choices accurately reflect the pragmatic aspects and convey appropriate additional information. These are called here the *rhetorical* concerns.

This paper describes how the program PAULINE (Planning And Uttering Language In Natural Environments) produces stylistically appropriate texts from a single story representation under various settings that model pragmatic circumstances.

PAULINE addresses simultaneously a wider range of problems than has been tried in any single language generation program before (with the possible exception of Clippinger [1974]). It contains about 12,000 lines of LISP code, and produces varied and sophisticated text. As is to be expected, no part of PAULINE provides a satisfactorily detailed solution to any problem; to a larger or smaller degree, each of the questions it addresses is solved by a set of simplified, somewhat ad hoc methods. In fact, some methods have been studied in much greater detail by other NLP researchers. Others remain as projects for the future.

However, this does not invalidate the content of the work. *This research uncovered two principal insights about the nature of language generation that do not depend directly on the details; they will hold for any language generator sophisticated enough to try to achieve a number of communicative goals in a single text. While the details of any particular module will not be defended too hard, nor even the exact extent of each module, the following will be defended to the end: the existence of a level of organization mediating between communicative goals and generator decisions, containing entities called here rhetorical goals; and the monitoring of the modules' operation in an interleaved planning-realization regime. The lessons learned here are going to apply to any large and complex enough generator — human or computer.*

Pragmatic Characteristics

PAULINE contains pragmatic representations of the characteristics of speaker-hearer interactions. These pragmatic characteristics are described in the following section (Hovy 1990, 160–161, 163):

In order to study the relationship between pragmatic considerations and computer language generation, one requires something concrete enough to program. To characterize the pragmatics of its conversation, PAULINE used a list of features. . . . The precise names and values of these features are not a serious claim; the (pragmatic!) justification is that they are the kinds of features necessary for language generation. Any language processing program addressing these questions will have features that, on some level, resemble them. In this representation of pragmatics, each feature was given a fixed number of possible values, usually lying on a scale. In a few cases, features were conflated and the result merely given a set of distinct values; this could eventually be refined. PAULINE's characterization of the *conversation setting* and *interlocutor characteristics* is:

*conversational atmosphere (setting):
   — time: much, some, little;
   — tone: formal, informal, festive;
   — conditions: good, noisy;

*speaker:
- — knowledge of the topic: expert, student, novice;
- — interest in the topic: high, low;
- — opinions of the topic: good, neutral, bad;
- — emotional state: happy, angry, calm;

*hearer:
- — knowledge of the topic: expert, student, novice;
- — interest in the topic: high, low;
- — opinions of the topic: good, neutral, bad;
- — language ability: high, low;
- — emotional state: happy, angry, calm;

*speaker-hearer relationship:
- — depth of acquaintance: friends, acquaintances, strangers;
- — relative social status: dominant, equal, subordinate;
- — emotion: like, neutral, dislike.

In addition, PAULINE can have the following *interpersonal goals:*

*hearer:
- — affect hearer's knowledge: teach, neutral, confuse;
- — affect hearer's opinions of topic: switch, none, reinforce;
- — involve hearer in the conversation: involve, neutral, repel;
- — affect hearer's emotional state: anger, neutral, calm;
- — affect hearer's goals: activate, neutral, deactivate;

*speaker-hearer relationship:
- — affect hearer's emotion toward speaker: respect, like, dislike;
- — affect relative status: dominant, equal, subordinate;
- — affect interpersonal distance: intimate, close, distant.

PAULINE uses the following stylistic rhetorical goals, with values along the indicated ranges:

- — formality (highfalutin, normal, colloquial): highfalutin language is used for speeches;
- — simplicity (simple, normal, complex): simple text has short sentences and easy words;
- — timidity (timid, reckless): willingness to spend time to consider including opinions;
- — partiality (impartial, implicit, explicit): how explicitly you state your opinions;
- — detail (details only, interpretations, both): too many details can be boring to nonexperts;
- — haste (pressured, unplanned, somewhat planned, planned): when there's little time;

— force (forceful, normal, quiet): forceful text is energetic and driving;
— floridity (dry, neutral, flowery): flowery text contains unusual words;
— color (facts only, with color): colorful text includes examples and idioms;
— personal reference (two ranges, for speaker and hearer): amount of direct reference to the interlocutors;
— open-mindedness (narrow-minded, open-minded): willingness to consider new topics;
— respect (four values): being arrogant, respectful, neutral, or cajoling.

Of course, it is impossible to list all possible styles. Every speaker has an idiosyncratic set of techniques, often tailored to particular hearers, for using language to achieve his or her interpersonal goals. Thus, this work should not be interpreted as claiming to describe exhaustively any language user's stylistic knowledge. Rather, it is intended as a description of the general *function of style* in a generator — the expression of rhetorical goals, which in turn serve the speaker's general communicative goals in the text; and of useful *method of definition of style* — as constraints on the decisions the generator has to make.

Architecture

The following succinct description of the architecture of PAULINE is provided (Hovy 1990, 169–170):

PAULINE has the architecture shown in [Figure 5.1]. Its input is represented in a standard case-frame-type language based on conceptual dependency (Schank, 1972, 1975; Schank & Abelson, 1977) and is embedded in a property-inheritance network (see Bobrow & Winograd, 1977; Charniak, Riesbeck, & McDermott, 1980). The shantytown example consists of about 120 elements. No intermediate representation (say, one that varies depending on the desired slant and style) is created. Its grammar is described in Hovy (1988). The program consists of about 12,000 lines of T, a scheme-like dialect of LISP developed at Yale.

Interpretation

The following section provides a conceptual analysis of the problem of text interpretation in general and examples of PAULINE's interpretative behavior (Hovy 1990, 175–178, italics added):

In [the following] example, PAULINE produces a number of versions describing a hypothetical primary election between Carter and Kennedy during the 1980 Democratic Presidential nomination race. In the election, Kennedy narrows Carter's lead. The underlying representation comprises about 80 distinct

FIGURE 5.1
Program Architecture

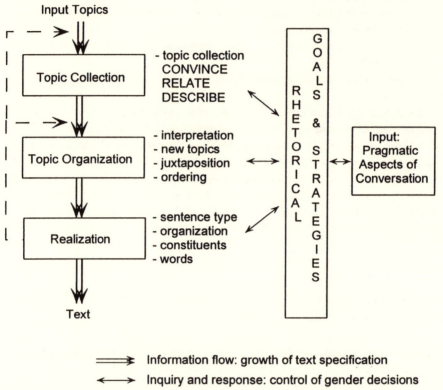

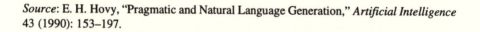

Source: E. H. Hovy, "Pragmatic and Natural Language Generation," *Artificial Intelligence* 43 (1990): 153–197.

units. When PAULINE is given as input the outcome for each candidate, straight-forward generation produces:

(f) IN THE PRIMARY ON 20 FEBRUARY CARTER GOT 1850 VOTES. KENNEDY GOT 2185.

However, PAULINE can notice that both outcomes relate to the same primary, and can say instead:

(g) IN THE PRIMARY ON 20 FEBRUARY, KENNEDY BEAT CARTER BY 335 VOTES.

(or any of a number of similar sentences using "beat," "win," and "lose"). But why stop there? If PAULINE examines the input further, it can notice that Carter's current delegate count is greater than Kennedy's, that this was also the case before the primary, and that this primary is part of a series that culminates in the final election, the nomination. In other words, PAULINE can recognize that what happened in this primary was:

(h) IN THE PRIMARY ON 20 FEBRUARY, KENNEDY NARROWED CARTER'S LEAD BY GETTING 2185 VOTES TO HIS 1850.

If we want good text from our generators, we have to give them the ability to recognize that "beat" or "lose" or "narrow lead" can be used instead of only the straightforward sentences (f).

This ability is more than a simple grouping of the two outcomes. It is an act of generator-directed inference, of interpretation, forming out of the two topics a new topic, perhaps one that does not even exist in memory yet. And the new topic is not simply a generator construct, but is a valid concept in memory. The act of determining that "beat" is appropriate *is* the act of interpreting the input as an instance of BEAT — denying this is to imply that "beat" can logically be used where BEAT is not appropriate, which is a contradiction. This is not an obvious point; one could hold that the task of finding "beat" to satisfy a syntactic or pragmatic goal is a legitimate generator function, whereas the task of instantiating it and incorporating it into memory is not. However, it is clearly inefficient for a generator to interpret its input, say it, and then simply forget it again! — especially when there is no principled reason why generator inferences should be distinct from other memory processes.

Thus, after interpretation, the newly built instance of the concept should be added to the story representation, where it can also be used by other processes, or by the generator the next time it tells the story. In this way the content of memory can change as a result of generation. This is consistent with the fact that you often understand a topic better after you have told someone about it: the act of generating has caused you to make explicit and to remember some information you didn't have before.

Immediately, this view poses the question: *which process is responsible for making these inferences?* The two possible positions on this issue reflect the amount of work one expects the generator to do. According to the strict minimalist position — a position held by most, if not all, generator builders today — the generator's responsibility is to produce text that faithfully mirrors the input topics with minimal deviation; each sentence-level input topic produces a distinct output sentence (though perhaps conjoined with or subordinated to another). This inflexible attitude gave rise to the JUDGE texts (a) and (b). To circumvent this problem, in practice, most generator builders employ in their programs a number of special-purpose techniques, such as sophisticated sentence specialists that are sensitive to the subsequent input topics. This is a tacit acknowledgment that the strict position does not hold. However, on renouncing the hard-line position, one must face the question *how much generator-directed inference are you prepared to do?*

I do not believe that a simple answer can be given to this question. The issue here is economic: a tradeoff exists between the time and effort required to do interpretation (which includes finding candidate interpretations, making them, and deciding on one) on the one hand, and the importance of flowing, good text on the other. Greater expense in time and effort produces better text. Thus pragmatic criteria are appropriate for treating this question. Hence a reasonable answer is *I'll do as much inference as I can do, given the available time, the pragmatic constraints on what I want the hearer to know, and the richness of my memory and my lexicon.* Of these three factors, the most difficult is clearly the pragmatic constraints on what the hearer is to be told. When does the hearer need to know the details of the topic? What is the effect of saying only interpretations? Or of saying both? The answer can be summarized as: if you can trust the hearer to make the interpretations himself, then all you need say are the details. Thus, if the hearer is a political pundit who is following the nomination race with interest, then clearly (f) is better, since he or she can draw the conclusion without difficulty, and, in addition, now has precise numerical information. If, in contrast, the hearer has only minimal knowledge about or interest in the nomination procedure, then (h) is better, since it removes the burden of details and the task of doing the interpretation. What must you say, however, if the hearer is interested and has a limited amount of knowledge — say, he or she is a student of the political process — or is knowledgeable but unlikely to make the right interpretation — say, he or she is a strong Kennedy supporter, whereas you are pro-Carter? In both these cases you must ensure that the hearer understands how you expect him or her to interpret the facts. So you give the details *and* the interpretations:

(i)   KENNEDY NARROWED CARTER'S LEAD IN THE PRIMARY ON 20 FEBRUARY. HE GOT 2185 VOTES AND CARTER GOT 1850.

These considerations can be stated as rules, using the terms defined above to characterize the pragmatic aspects of conversations and the goals of speakers. PAULINE uses these rules to activate the rhetorical goal *detail* that controls the level of detail of topics generated. The goal takes one of the values *details, interpretations, all* (both details and interpretations):

—   Set the goal's value to *details* if the hearer is likely to understand the details or wants to hear the details. This rule bears on information about the hearer: Is the hearer's knowledge level marked *expert*; or is the hearer's interest level marked *high*?
—   Otherwise, set it to *all* if the hearer is likely to make the wrong interpretations of the details, that is, when the hearer's knowledge level is marked *student* or *novice*; the atmosphere (time) is not marked *little*; and the hearer's

sympathies and antipathies for the central topic of the conversation are not the opposite of the speaker's.

— Otherwise, set it to *interpretations*.

In addition to these considerations, the value of the goal can be affected by the desire not to upset the hearer:

— Then, set the value to *interpretations* if it is better to avoid painful topics, to ensure that painful aspects (the details, the interpretation, or the inferences used to make it) can simply be left out. This rule translates as follows: Is speaker-hearer depth of acquaintance marked *strangers*, or is speaker-hearer relative social status marked *subordinate*, or is desired effect of hearer's emotion toward speaker marked *like*, or is desired effect of interpersonal distance marked *close*, or is desired effect on hearer's emotional state marked *calm*?

In summary, you must be as specific as the hearer's knowledge of the topic allows: if you are too specific he or she won't understand, and if you are too general you run the risk of seeming to hide things, or of being uncooperative. In the first case, you violate the goal to be intelligible, and in the second, you violate the goal to avoid unacceptable implications. In either case, you violate Grice's maxim of quantity to say neither more nor less than is required (Grice, 1975).

Affect

It is interesting that PAULINE can process, within limits, the affective aspects of interpersonal communications. In the following section, the concepts and rules that guide PAULINE's affective behavior are described (Hovy 1990, 182–183):

In order to slant the text to fit the hearer's opinions, the speaker must be able to determine what the hearer is likely to find sympathetic, what he or she is likely to dislike, and what he or she is likely not to care about much. PAULINE uses three values of affect: GOOD, BAD and NEUTRAL. (Of course, *affect* here simply denotes something akin to "like." But even with this limited denotation, three values are sufficient to give the program interesting behavior. In this regard it is similar to the work on narrative summarization in Lehnert [1982].)

PAULINE's affects derive from two sources: provided by the user and defined as intrinsic to certain representation elements. To give PAULINE opinions, the user must specify one or more representation elements as *sympathies* or *antipathies*. (In PAULINE, this is simply implemented by having a sympathy and an antipathy list. Elements on these lists will be characterized as GOOD and BAD respectively.) The second source of affect is defined for those generic representation elements that carry some intrinsic affect in the example domain. For example, in neutral context, the concept ARREST is BAD, the university's goal to be reasonable and fair is GOOD, and all other concepts, such as STUDENTS and CONSTRUCTION, are NEUTRAL.

In order to compute an opinion about any arbitrary piece of input representation, PAULINE has the ability to combine its given affects and concepts' intrinsic affects and to propagate affect along relations to other concepts. Though their exact form obviously depends on the design of the representation, the basic rules are:

(1) affect is preserved when combined with NEUTRAL;
(2) like affects combine to GOOD;
(3) unlike affects combine to BAD;
(4) affect inverts when propagated along certain relations (e.g., the *patient* of a BAD act is GOOD). A special rule for affect propagation is defined for each such relation.

Partiality and Impartiality

A conceptual analysis of the conditions for the expression of partial and impartial opinions is presented, and the implementation of this analysis by a set of rules in PAULINE is discussed in the following section (Hovy 1990, 182–190):

When should the speaker exhibit partiality? In general, since his or her sympathies and antipathies reflect so accurately the speaker's disposition toward the world, any opinion with which the hearer disagrees implies distance between them — perhaps even censure on the part of the speaker. Thus, to simplify, when the speaker's opinion agrees with the hearer's, expressing it will tend to make them closer; when it disagrees, expressing it may cause problems. Furthermore, partiality can be expressed explicitly, using clauses that state the speaker's opinion, or implicitly, using techniques such as phrasal juxtaposition and stress words. The rules PAULINE uses to activate its rhetorical goal of partiality are:

(1) Set the value of the goal to *explicit* if the speaker's and hearer's affects for the topic agree and desired effect on hearer's emotion toward speaker is marked *like*; or desired effect on interpersonal distance is marked *close*; or tone is marked *informal*.
(2) Set it to *implicit* if the speaker's and hearer's affects for the topic agree and desired effect on interpersonal distance is marked *distant*, since being lukewarm about the agreement with the hearer separates them; or speaker-hearer relative social status is marked *dominant*, for the same reason; or desire to

involve hearer is marked *repel*, that is, if the speaker does not want to make the hearer too involved in the conversation.

(3) Otherwise, set it to *impartial* if their affects agree, or if their affects disagree and desired effect on hearer's opinion is marked *none*, hearer's knowledge level is marked *expert*, and speaker's knowledge level is marked *student* or *novice*, and desired effect on hearer's emotion toward speaker is marked *respect* or *like*, since when the speaker cares about an expert hearer's opinion, he or she will not want to exhibit partiality and lack of knowledge.

(4) Set the value of the goal to *explicit* if the speaker's and hearer's affects for the topic disagree and desired effect on hearer's opinion is marked *switch*; or desired effect on hearer's emotional state is marked *anger*; or desired effect on hearer's emotion toward speaker is marked *dislike*; or desired effect on interpersonal distance is marked *distant*.

(5) Otherwise, set it to *implicit* if their affects disagree and desired effect on hearer's opinion is marked *switch*; or desire to involve hearer is marked *involve*; or relative social status is marked *subordinate* (that is, when the hearer is subordinate to the speaker).

Having determined a value for this goal of partiality, PAULINE uses the following strategies of style that act as criteria at decision points to make text partial (both *explicit* and *implicit*):

(1) *topic inclusion*: include explicit expressions of opinion (if *explicit*)
(2) *topic organization*: make appropriate interpretations of topics, as discussed below (if *implicit*)
(3) *topic/phrase organization*: juxtapose topics in affect-imputing phrases (*explicit* and *implicit*)
(4) *sentence inclusion and organization*: include appropriate descriptive adjunct groups, adverbial and adjectival (*explicit*)
(5) *sentence constituent inclusion*: include appropriate affect-laden adjectives and adverbs; and include stress words (*explicit* and *implicit*)
(6) *word choice*: select nouns and verbs that carry affect (*explicit* and *implicit*)

In contrast, in order to make its text as impartial as possible, the program uses inverse strategies.

In the shantytown example of [Table 5.1], PAULINE is given three input topics (the building of the shanties, their being taken down, and Yale's permission for them to be rebuilt). When the program has the goal to switch the hearer's opinions to correspond to its own, it activates the CONVINCE topic collection plan. When PAULINE is speaking as a university supporter, the *good results* step of the plan causes it to collect, as additional topics, the university's offer of an alternative site for the shanties and the protesters' refusal to move, since these topics are (a) direct results of the building of the shanties and are (b) GOOD from the program's point of view, for they serve the university's goal to be lenient and

TABLE 5.1
Partiality

For Protesters	For University	Decision Strategy
[AS A REMINDER TO] YALE UNIVERSITY TO DIVEST FROM COMPANIES DOING BUSINESS IN SOUTH AFRICA,		interp: *support*
[A LARGE NUMBER OF] [CONCERNED] STUDENTS	IN APRIL, [A SMALL NUMBER OF] [ ] STUDENTS	adj choice: enhancer interp: *tactics*
ERECTED A SHANTYTOWN NAMED WINNIE MANDELA CITY ON BEINECKE PLAZA IN APRIL.	[TOOK OVER] BEINECKE PLAZA AND ERECTED A SHANTYTOWN NAMED WINNIE MANDELA CITY	topic: given in input
	[IN ORDER TO FORCE] YALE UNIVERSITY TO DIVEST FROM COMPANIES DOING BUSINESS IN SOUTH AFRICA.	interp: *coercion*
	YALE [REQUESTED] THAT THE STUDENTS BUILD IT ELSEWHERE, BUT THEY REFUSED TO LEAVE.	verb choice: leniency topic: pro-university
	SO THE UNIVERSITY GAVE IT PERMISSION TO EXIST UNTIL THE MEETING OF THE	topic: pro-university
	YALE CORPORATION, BUT [EVEN] AFTER THAT THEY [STILL] REFUSED TO MOVE.	adv choice: enhancer adv choice: enhancer topic: pro-university

142

Generated text	interp/annotation
[AT 5:30 AM ON APRIL 14,] [YALE HAD] OFFICIALS [DESTROY] IT; ALSO, AT THAT TIME, THE UNIVERSITY [HAD] THE POLICE ARREST 76 STUDENTS AFTER THE LOCAL COMMUNITY'S [HUGE] [OUTCRY].	interp: *abnormal-circ*
OFFICIALS [HAD TO] [DISASSEMBLE] THE SHANTYTOWN	interp: *coercion*
	verb choice: force
	topic: given in input
[ ]. FINALLY,	interp: *coercion*
	topic: pro-protesters
YALE PERMITTED THE STUDENTS TO RECONSTRUCT THE SHANTYTOWN	topic: pro-protesters
	interp: *support*
YALE, [BEING CONCILIATORY] TOWARD THE STUDENTS, [NOT ONLY] PERMITTED THEM TO, RECONSTRUCT IT [BUT ALSO] ANNOUNCED THAT A COMMISSION WOULD GO TO SOUTH AFRICA IN JULY TO STUDY THE SYSTEM OF APARTHEID.	interp: *conciliation*
	phrase juxta: enhancer
	topic: given in input
	phrase juxta: enhancer
	topic: pro-university

Source: E. H. Hovy, "Pragmatics and Natural Language Generation," *Artificial Intelligence* 43 (1990), 153–197. Reprinted with permisison of Elsevier Science Publishers.

show the protesters' intransigence. When on the other hand it is speaking as protester, the same step causes it to collect the item representing the students' arrest. Other steps of the plan provide other topics. Eventually, having performed the collection, PAULINE begins topic organization with the initial input and the topics it has collected.

[PAULINE] has limited inferential capability. It also has a list of rules that prescribe how the generator should proceed to find forms of expression for input topics with certain characteristics, and that indicate what aspects of these topics can be used to create an appropriate slant. The goals that activate these rules are called the *rhetorical goals of opinion*. When the program is given sympathies that oppose the hearer's sympathies, and when the pragmatic value for effect on hearer's opinion of the topic is *switch*, PAULINE activates these goals, which can be paraphrased as:

— *State outright* that our side is good and theirs is bad.
— Show how our side has *good goals*, by describing how (a) we help other people; (b) we want a solution to the conflict; and (c) our goals are good according to accepted standards.
— Explain how our side does *good actions* to achieve the goals: (a) the actions are not unreasonable or nasty; (b) they are good according to accepted standards; and (c) they are performed in the open.
— Specifically, describe our side's *response to the opponent*: (a) negotiations that have taken place and (b) how we have moderated our demands.
— Finally, show how *other people* believe that we are good, by describing (a) their active support and (b) their statements and recommendations to that effect.

A similar list exists for the inverse goal, to show how bad the opponents' side is. Both lists contain a large number of specific inferences and explicit suggestions for sentences. For example, a strategy to make the opponents look bad is:

— Show how *they are unreasonable*: (a) they started the whole affair; (b) they coerce others into doing things; (c) they have little support; (d) they don't seem to want a solution; (e) their demands/goals are beyond reasonable expectations; (f) they are only in it for their own good; (g) they are immoral, unfair; (h) they use distasteful/ugly tactics, misuse their rights, or overstep the bounds of propriety; (i) they disseminate false or misleading information about the dispute; (j) they have a hidden agenda; (k) they won't discuss/negotiate the issue; (l) they won't moderate their stance, are unconciliatory, intransigent.

These strategies are encoded as top-down interpretation inferences. They fire when the input sentence topics have characteristics that match their activation conditions; the left-hand sides are patterns of representation element types and their right-hand sides cause the generator to select the appropriate forms of expression. In somewhat more detail, the inferences *coercion* and *limited support* (see [Table 5.2]) can be paraphrased as (the terms in capitals are elements of the representation language; MTRANS denotes the act of transferring information; PTRANS the act of transferring physical objects; and ATRANS the act of transferring control over something; see Schank, 1972; Schank & Abelson, 1977):

— *Coercion*: they force their will on others (corresponding to the university speaker's "in order to force"):

IF the current topic is an ACTION,
    AND its affect is BAD,
    AND the action serves one of the opponent's goals,
    AND the goal's desire is to have some other party do some act,
THEN imply that the opponents force their will on them (using verbs and phrases such as "force," "make them do").

— *Limited support*: they claim to have more support than they have (corresponding to the university speaker's adjective "a small number"):

IF the current topic claims support (an MTRANS of a SUPPORT),
    AND the ACTOR's affect is BAD,
    AND the SUPPORT contains a number of people,
THEN minimize that number, by using adjectives such as "a small number," "a few."

Different inferences are applied at different times in the generation process. This depends on the kinds of effect they have on the processing and is controlled by the grammar. Inferences that call for the candidate topic(s) to be interpreted and completely replaced by other topics (such as interpreting a request as a coercion) are run during the topic organization phase; inferences that suggest appropriate adjectives ("a large number," "a small group") are run when noun phrases are built; those that prescribe specific verbs when predicates are constructed. . . . Thus, in addition to stressing affective concepts, a speaker can strengthen his or her case by imputing affect to neutral concepts too! This is, for example, what PAULINE does to produce

NOT ONLY DID YALE UNIVERSITY PERMIT THE STUDENTS TO REBUILD THE SHANTYTOWN, BUT YALE ANNOUNCED THAT A COMMISSION WOULD GO TO SOUTH AFRICA TO STUDY THE SYSTEM OF APARTHEID.

when defending the university (see [Table 5.1]). For PAULINE, the commission visit topic is simply NEUTRAL, whereas permission to rebuild, because it serves

TABLE 5.2
Case 1 (to an acquaintance): *colloquial, impartial, details, somewhat planned*

Text	Decision	Rhetorical Goal Value
Topic: central topic		
[ ] CARTER AND KENNEDY WERE	RELATE plan	*colloquial*
THE CANDIDATES IN A PRIMARY	no adjuncts before	
[IN MICHIGAN] [ON 20 FEBRUARY].	adjuncts after subject	*colloquial, planned*
Topic: result	RELATE plan	*impartial*
CARTER [LOST]	neutral verb	*impartial, details*
TO KENNEDY BY [1335] VOTES.	neutral details	*impartial*
Topic: outcome with good affect for Kennedy	RELATE plan	
AT PRESENT, KENNEDY		
HAS A BETTER CHANCE	informal word	*colloquial*
OF [GETTING] THE NOMINATION	elide *he had*	*colloquial*
THAN [ ] BEFORE.	RELATE plan	*impartial*
Topic: outcome with good affect for Carter	separate sentence	*colloquial*
CARTER IS ALSO CLOSER	informal word	*colloquial*
TO [GETTING] THE	elide *he was*	*colloquial*
NOMINATION THAN [ ] BEFORE.	RELATE plan	
Topic: actor's goals (twice)		
BOTH CARTER AND KENNEDY [WANT]	informal verb	*colloquial*
TO [GET] THE NOMINATION	informal verb	*colloquial*

Source: E. H. Hovy, "Pragmatics and Natural Language Generation," *Artificial Intelligence* 43 (1990): 191. Reprinted with permission of Elsevier Science Publishers.

the goal to be reasonable (which is intrinsically GOOD) is GOOD. When juxta-posed in this way, *both* sentences seem GOOD for Yale — exactly what PAULINE wants.

The juxtaposition of topics is controlled by the active rhetorical goals of opin-ion. In the shantytown example, for instance, the program's first goal is to intro-duce the topic. Its topic collection strategies provide it with two topics (the shan-ty construction and the protesters' intention) that are related by a SUBGOAL-TO relation. As at any decision point, the active rhetorical strategies of style are queried: should the relation between the two topics be used to conjoin them into a compound sentence? The answer is *yes*, since the relevant topic organization strategy, activated for both *explicit* and *implicit* values of partiality, calls for the use of affect-imputing enhancer and mitigator phrases. What is an appropriate way to express a SUBGOAL-TO relation? Here the inferences of opinion come into play, making decisions about the appropriateness of various interpretations of the two topics and their relationship. When sympathetic toward the university, one inference that matches the construction and its goal, which has the desired state that Yale divest from the companies, is that of *coercion*, described above. This strategy spawns the instruction to say a newly-formed interpretation, CAUSE-TO-DO, with the protesters' intent as attached topic, and the conjunc-tion "in order to force." In contrast, when PAULINE is speaking as a protester, the strategy *we are lenient, offer passive resistance* causes it to join the topics using the phrase "as a reminder to." (When the program has no opinions, it would simply use a neutral phrase such as "in order to" or "so as to.") All these phrases are in the lexicon, indexed in a discrimination net linked to the relation SUB-GOAL-TO.

Nouns and verbs often carry affective value themselves. The words in PAULINE's lexicon are organized in discrimination nets to provide enhancing and mitigating alternatives when required. For example, the representation prim-itive MTRANS indexes to, amongst others, the verbs "order," "tell," "ask," and "request"; and DECONSTRUCT to "tear down," "disassemble," and "remove." See [Table 5.1].

A Further Example of Performance

In the following section, another interesting example of PAULINE's pragmatic generation of language is provided (Hovy 1990, 191–192):

In summary, compare PAULINE's generation of the Carter-Kennedy example under three pragmatically different scenarios. In all three cases, the input is the same; the differences in the text result from the different values for the active rhetorical goals, which result from the different initial pragmatic settings. Only the effects of the rhetorical goals of formality, detail, partiality and haste will be discussed here (see Hovy [1987] for more details).

Case 1. Neither interlocutor has opinions about the topic (causing partiality to be set to *impartial*); both have the usual knowledge of the electoral process (making detail be *details*); the level of formality is *colloquial*; and when the program is given enough time, haste is activated with the value *somewhat planned*. The result appears in [Table 5.2].

Case 2. The hearer is a *friend* and social *equal* (therefore again *colloquial* formality) who is not as expert as the sibling (i.e., knowledge level is *student*, which makes detail be *details and interpretations*). But now both interlocutors have opinions: PAULINE's sympathy is for Kennedy and the hearer's is for Carter (so that partiality is *implicit*). The program is given as much time (mainly to make interpretations) as it needs: haste is *planned*. The result appears in [Table 5.3].

Case 3. PAULINE is a Carter supporter and is speaking to its boss, an irascible Kennedy man. They are making a long-distance telephone call, which gives the program *little* time and makes conversational conditions *noisy* (activating the haste goal with the value *pressured*). Furthermore, the program is *distant* from its boss, does not wish to anger him (desired emotional effect is *calm down*), and still wants to make him feel socially *dominant* (resulting in *implicit* partiality and *interpretations* for detail). But to its boss ([Table 5.4]), the program says nothing!

This text came as a surprise. Investigation showed that the lack of time prevented any of the strategies for implicitly stating opinions from being applied: no topic collection plan was activated; no search for mitigating interpretations took place; the lack of a second topic meant no topic juxtaposition was possible; no rhetorical goals of opinion were present to guide mitigating adverb and adjective selection and appropriate word choice. Therefore, the goal to present the topic only in mitigated (implicit opinion) form couldn't be satisfied, and no sentence could be generated.

Limitations

In the following section, PAULINE is evaluated from several perspectives, with emphasis on the general applicability to other language generation systems of the two basic assumptions underlying theory and performance of the PAULINE system (Hovy 1990, 193):

The question "why and how is it that we say the same thing in different ways to different people, or even to the same person in different circumstances?" is interesting from a number of perspectives. From a cognitive perspective, it highlights speakers' goals and personal interrelationships in communication; from a linguistic perspective, it raises interesting questions about the information content of language; and from an engineering-AI perspective, it illustrates the need for principled reasons by which a program that can realize the same input in various ways can make its selections.

TABLE 5.3

Case 2 (to a friend): *colloquial, implicit, all (details and interpretations), planned*

Text	Decision	Rhetorical Goal Value
Topic: results with good affect for Kennedy	CONVINCE plan	*implicit*
[ ] KENNEDY	no adjuncts before	*colloquial*
[DIMINISHED] CARTER'S [LEAD]	interpretation	*all, planned*
BY [GETTING]	informal verb	*colloquial*
[ALL OF]	enhance adj	*implicit*
[21850] VOTES	details	*all*
[IN THE PRIMARY] [IN MICHIGAN]	adjuncts after subject	*colloquial*
Topic: reminding	indexed off interp	*planned*
IN A SIMILAR CASE, CARTER DECREASED	reminding	*implicit, planned*
UDALL'S LEAD IN A PRIMARY		
IN 1976, AND HE [EASILY]	enhancer adv	*implicit*
[TROUNCED] UDALL TO BE NOMINATED	enhancer verb	*implicit*
BY [2600] DELEGATES	details	*all*
Topic: outcome with good affect for Kennedy	CONVINCE plan	*implicit*
[I AM REAL GLAD THAT]	informal opinion	*colloquial, explicit*
KENNEDY IS [NOW] CLOSER TO	adjunct after, informal	*colloquial*
[GETTING THE NOMINATION THAN	informal verb	*colloquial*
[ ] BEFORE.	elide *he was*	*colloquial*

Source: E. H. Hovy, "Pragmatics and Natural Language Generation," *Artificial Intelligence* 43 (1990): 153–197. Reprinted with permisison of Elsevier Science Publishers.

TABLE 5.4
Case 3 (to the boss): *colloquial, implicit, interpretations, pressured*

Text	Decision	Rhetorical Goal Value
Topic: results and outcomes for Carter	CONVINCE plan	*implicit*
. . . .	no time for mitigation	*pressured*

Source: E. H. Hovy, "Pragmatics and Natural Language Generation," *Artificial Intelligence* 43 (1990): 153–197. Reprinted with permission of Elsevier Science Publishers.

As described in this paper, the answer deals with the pragmatic nature of communication — a big and complex field of study. In order to begin to study how pragmatics is used in generation, a number of assumptions about plausible types of speaker goals and the relevant characteristics of hearers and of conversational settings must be made. The specific pragmatic features used by PAULINE are but a first step. They are the types of factors that play a role in conversation; no claims are made about their literal veracity. Similarly, the strategies PAULINE uses to link its pragmatic features to the actual generator decisions, being dependent on the definitions of the features, are equally primitive; again, no strong claims are made about their existence in people in exactly the form shown. However, in even such a simple theory as this, certain lessons emerge, and these lessons, I believe, hold true no matter how sophisticated the eventual theory is. The lessons pertain primarily to the organization of pragmatic information in generation: the fact that interpersonal and situational information and goals are too general to be of immediate use; the resulting fact that intermediate strategies, here called rhetorical strategies, are required to guide generation; the fact that, in a model of generation that incorporates these goals, rhetorical planning and realization must be interleaved processes, where the interleaving takes place at the choice points.

The study of language generation by computer has traditionally been divided into two questions: *what shall I say?* and *how shall I say it?* The aim of this work is to illustrate the importance of a third question: *why should I say it?* If generators do not face up to this question, they will never be able to address the other two satisfactorily.

COMMENTARY

Pragmatics and Computation

The PAULINE program is an important contribution to artificial intelligence approaches that seek the emulation of human capacities for pragmatic language generation. The principles that enable PAULINE to adjust its knowledge and rhetorical style to different audiences, goals, and purposes are generalizable to other programs and other contexts.

The expansion of computational principles and programs to three additional areas of language pragmatics seems warranted: conversational norms, common ground enabling conversations, and speech acts.

Computation and Conversational Norms

The area of conversational norms (Grice, 1975) may, in some respects, be especially amenable to computational approaches, simply because clear conversational norms and stipulations can be represented as production rules.

Computation and Common Grounds

In contrast to the precision of conversational norms, the variability of human conversation modes and contents constitutes a more formidable challenge to computational competencies. The constituents of linguistic common ground that permit effective human communication need to be established; it is these constituents and their concatenation that an expert computer conversationalist would need to emulate.

Computation and Speech Acts

The area of speech acts (Austin, 1962; Searle, 1969) comprises two levels of difficulty for computational approaches. Speech acts conveying meanings that are explicit, simple, and univocal in their implications can be computationally emulated more readily than speech acts conveying multiple messages, some explicit and some implicit, contradictory at different levels, with open-ended interpretations.

Bibliography

Abbey, E. 1971. *Desert solitaire*. New York: Ballantine.

Agre, P. E. 1985. *Routines* (AI Memo 828). Cambridge, MA: MIT Press.

Agre, P. E. 1989. The dynamic structure of everyday life. Ph.D. dissertation, MIT.

Anderson, J. R., C. F. Boyle, and B. J. Reiser. 1985. Intelligent tutoring systems. *Science* 228: 456–462.

Anderson, J. R., R. Farrell, and R. Sauers. 1984. Learning to program in LISP. *Cognitive Science* 8: 87–129.

Austin, J. L. 1962. *How to do things with words*. Oxford: Oxford University Press.

Backus, J. 1978. Can programming be liberated from the von Neumann style? *Communications of the ACM* 21: 613–641.

Barr, A., and E. Feigenbaum. 1982. *The handbook of artificial intelligence*. Los Altos, CA: Morgan Kaufmann.

Barwise, J. 1986. The situation in logic II: Conditionals and conditional information. In *On conditionals*, ed. E. C. Traugott, C. A. Ferguson, and J. S. Reilly. Cambridge, MA: Cambridge University Press.

Barwise, J., and J. Etchemendy. 1989. Model-theoretic semantics. In *Foundations of cognitive science*, ed. M. Posner. Cambridge, MA: MIT Press.

Barwise, J., and J. Etchemendy. 1990. Information, infons, and inference. In *Situation theory and its applications*, ed. R. Cooper, K. Mukai, and J. Perry. Chicago: University of Chicago Press.

Barwise, J., and J. Etchemendy. 1991. Visual information and valid reasoning. In *Visualization in teaching and learning mathematics*, ed. W. Zimmerman and S. Cunningham. Washington, DC: Mathematical Association of America.

Barwise, J., and J. Etchemendy. In press. Visual information and valid reasoning. In *Model theoretic semantics*, ed. W. Zimmerman. Washington, DC: Mathematical Association of America.

Barwise, J., and J. Perry. 1983. *Situations and attitudes*. Cambridge, MA: MIT Press.

Basler, R. P., ed. 1953. *Collected works of Abraham Lincoln*. New Brunswick, NJ: Rutgers University Press.

Becker, J. D. 1973. A model for the encoding of experiential information. In *Computer models of thought and language*, ed. R. C. Schank and K. M. Colby, pp. 396–435. San Francisco: Freeman.

Bobrow, D. G., and T. Winograd. 1977. An overview of KRL: A knowledge representation language. *Cognitive Science* 1: 3–46.

Bobrow, D. G., T. Winograd et al. 1977. Experience with KRL-0: One cycle of a knowledge representation language. *Proceedings IJCAI-77*, pp. 213–222. Cambridge, MA.

Brewer, W. F., and A. Samarapungavan. 1991. Child theories versus scientific theories: Differences in reasoning or differences in knowledge? In *Cognition and the symbolic processes: Applied and ecological perspectives*, ed. R. R. Hoffman and D. S. Palermo. Hillsdale, NJ: Erlbaum.

Brooks, R. A. 1986. A robust layered control system for a mobile robot. *IEEE Transactions on Robotics and Automation* 2: 14–23.

Brown, A. L., and J. C. Campione. 1985. Three faces of transfer: Implications for early competence, individual differences, and instruction. In *Advances in developmental psychology*, ed. M. Lamb, A. L. Brown, and B. Rogoff. Hillsdale, NJ: Erlbaum.

Brown, R. 1977. Use of analogy to achieve new expertise. Ph.D. dissertation, MIT.

Bruner, J. S., J. J. Goodnow, and G. A. Austin. 1956. *A study of thinking*. New York: NY Science Editions.

Burstein, M. 1986. Concept formation by incremental analogical reasoning and debugging. In *Machine learning: An artificial intelligence approach*, ed. R. S. Michalski, J. G. Carbonell, and T. M. Mitchell, pp. 351–370. Los Altos, CA: Morgan Kaufmann.

Burstein, M., and B. Adelson. 1987. Analogical learning: Mapping and integrating partial mental models. *Program of the Ninth Annual Conference of the Cognitive Science Society*. Hillsdale, NJ: Erlbaum.

Carbonell, J. G. 1981. Invariance hierarchies in metaphor interpretation. *Proceedings Third Annual Meeting of the Cognitive Science Society*, pp. 292–295. Berkeley, CA.

Carbonell, J. G. 1982. Metaphor: An inescapable phenomenon in natural-language comprehension. In *Strategies for natural language processing*, ed. W. G. Lehnert and M. H. Ringle, pp. 415–435. Hillsdale, NJ: Erlbaum.

Carbonell, J. G. 1983a. Derivational analogy in problem solving and knowledge acquisition. *Proceedings International Machine Learning Workshop*, pp. 12–18. Monticello, IL.

Carbonell, J. G. 1983b. Learning by analogy: Formulating and generalizing plans from past experience. In *Machine learning: An artificial intelligence approach*, ed. R. S. Michalski, J. G. Carbonell, and T. M. Mitchell, pp. 137–162. Palo Alto, CA: Tioga.

Carbonell, J. G. 1986. Derivational analogy: A theory of reconstructive problem solving and expertise acquisition. In *Machine learning: An artificial intelligence approach*, ed. R. S. Michalski, J. G. Carbonell, and T. M. Mitchell, pp. 371–392. Los Altos, CA: Morgan Kaufman.

Carey, S. 1985. *Conceptual change in childhood*. Cambridge, MA: MIT Press.

Case, R. 1974. Structures and strictures: Some functional limitations on the course of cognitive growth. *Cognitive Psychology* 6: 544–573.

Catrambone, R., and K. J. Holyoak. 1990. Overcoming contextual limitations on problem solving transfer. *Journal of Experimental Psychology: Learning, Memory and Cognition* 15: 1147–1156.

Chapman, D., and P. E. Agre. 1987. Abstract reasoning as emergent from concrete activity. In *Reasoning about action and plans: Proceedings of the 1986 workshop*, ed. M. P. Georgeff and A. L. Lansky. Los Altos, CA: Morgan Kaufmann.

Charniak, E., C. K. Riesbeck, and D. V. McDermott. 1980. *Artificial intelligence programming*. Hillsdale, NJ: Erlbaum.

Cheng, P. W., and L. R. Novick. 1990a. A probabilistic contrast model of causal induction. *Journal of Personality and Social Psychology* 58: 545–567.

Cheng, P. W., and L. R. Novick. 1990b. Where is the bias in causal attribution? In *Lines of thought: Reflections on the psychology of thinking*, ed. K. Gilhooly, M. Keane, R. Logie, and G. Erdos, pp. 181–197. Chichester: Wiley.

Cheng, P. W., and L. R. Novick. 1991. Causes versus enabling conditions. *Cognition* 40: 83–120.

Clancey, W. J. 1979. Dialogue management for rule-based tutorials. *Proceedings IJCAI-79*, pp. 155–161. Tokyo, Japan

Clement, J. 1983. Observed methods for generating analogies in scientific problem solving. *Proceedings Annual Meeting of the American Educational Research Association*. Montreal, Canada.

Clippinger, J. H. 1974. A discourse speaking program as a preliminary theory of discourse behavior and a limited theory of psychoanalytic discourse. Ph.D. dissertation, University of Pennsylvania.

Conover, W. J. 1980. *Practical non-parametric statistics*. New York: Wiley.

Cruse, D. 1986. *Lexical semantics*. Cambridge: Cambridge University Press.

Cussins, A. 1990. The connectionist construction of concepts. In *The philosophy of artificial intelligence*, ed. M. Boden. Oxford: Oxford University Press.

Dennett, D. C. 1987. *The intentional stance*. Cambridge, MA: MIT Press.

Dreyfus, H. L. 1979. *What computers can't do: The limits of artificial intelligence* (rev. ed.). New York: Harper & Row.

Dreyfus, H. L. 1981. From micro-worlds to knowledge representation: AI at an impasse. In *Mind design: Philosophy, psychology, artificial intelligence*, ed. J. Haugeland. Cambridge, MA: MIT Press.

Dunbar, K., and D. Klahr. 1989. Developmental differences in scientific discovery strategies. In *Complex information processing: The impact of Herbert A. Simon*, ed. D. Klahr and K. Kotovsky. Hillsdale, NJ: Erlbaum.

Dunbar, K., and C. D. Schunn. 1990. The temporal nature of scientific discovery: The roles of priming and analogy. In *Proceedings of the Twelfth Annual Conference of the Cognitive Science Society*, pp. 93–100. Hillsdale, NJ: Erlbaum.

Duncker, K. 1945. On problem solving. *Psychology Monographs* 58, No. 270.

Dyer, M. G. 1983a. *In-depth understanding*. Cambridge, MA: MIT Press.

Dyer, M. G. 1983b. Understanding stories through morals and remindings. *Proceedings IJCAI-83*, pp. 75–77. Karlsruhe, FRG.

Erman, L., F. Hayes-Roth, V. Lesser, and D. R. Reddy. 1980. Hearsay-II speech understanding system. *Computer Survey* 12: 224–225.

Evans, G. 1982. *The varieties of reference*. Oxford: Oxford University Press.

Evans, J. St. B. T., J. L. Barston, and P. Pollard. 1983. On the conflict between logic and belief in syllogistic reasoning. *Memory & Cognition* 11: 295–306.

Evans, T. G. 1968. A program for the solution of a class of geometric analogy intelligence test questions. In *Semantic information processing*, ed. M. Minsky, pp. 271–353. Cambridge, MA: MIT Press.

Fagin, R., and J. Y. Halpern. 1985. Belief, awareness, and limited reasoning. *Proceedings IJCAI-85*, pp. 491–501. Los Angeles, CA.

Falkenhainer, B., K. D. Forbus, and D. Gentner. 1986. The structure-mapping engine. *Proceedings AAAI-86*, pp. 272–277. Philadelphia, PA.

Falkenhainer, B., K. D. Forbus, and D. Gentner. 1987. The structure-mapping engine: Algorithm and examples. Technical Report UIUCDCS-R-87-1361. Urbana, IL: University of Illinois, Department of Computer Science.

Falkenhainer, B., K. D. Forbus, and D. Gentner. 1989/90. The structure-mapping engine: Algorithms and examples. *Artificial Intelligence* 41: 1–63.

Faries, J., and B. Reiser. 1988. Access and use of previous solutions in a problem solving situation. *Proceedings Tenth Annual Conference of the Cognitive Science Society*, pp. 433–439. Montreal, Canada.

Fay, A. L., D. Klahr, and K. Dunbar. 1990. Are there developmental milestones in scientific reasoning? *Proceedings of the Twelfth Annual Conference of the Cognitive Science Society*, pp. 333–339. Hillsdale, NJ: Erlbaum.

Fodor, J. A., and Z. W. Pylyshyn. 1981. How direct is visual perception? *Cognition* 9: 139–196.

Genesereth, M. R., and N. J. Nilsson. 1987. *Logical foundations of artificial intelligence*. San Mateo, CA: Morgan Kaufmann.

Gentner, D. 1983. Structure-mapping: A theoretical framework for analogy. *Cognitive Science* 7: 155–170.

Gentner, D. 1989. The mechanisms of analogical reasoning. In *Similarity and analogical reasoning*, ed. S. Vosniadou and A. Ortony, pp. 199–241. New York: Cambridge University Press.

Gentner, D., and D. R. Gentner. 1983. Flowing waters or teeming crowds: Mental models of electricity. In *Mental Models*, ed. D. Gentner and A. L. Stevens, pp. 99–129. Hillsdale, NJ: Erlbaum.

Gentner, D., and R. Landers. 1985. Analogical reminding: A good match is hard to find. *Proceedings International Conference on Systems, Man, and Cybernetics*. Tucson, AZ.

Gholson, B., M. Levine, and S. Phillips. 1972. Hypotheses, strategies, and stereotypes in discrimination learning. *Journal of Experimental Child Psychology* 13: 423–446.

Gick, M. L., and K. J. Holyoak. 1980. Analogical problem solving. *Cognitive Psychology* 12: 306–355.

Gick, M. L., and K. J. Holyoak. 1983. Schema induction and analogic transfer. *Cognitive Psychology* 15: 1–38.

Gilovich, T. 1981. Seeing the past in the present: The effect of associations to familliar events on judgments and decisions. *Journal of Personality and Social Psychology* 40: 797–808.

Greiner, R. 1985. Learning by understanding analogies. Ph.D. dissertation, Stanford University.

Greiner, R. 1988. Learning by understanding analogies. *Artificial Intelligence* 35: 81–125.

Grice, H. P. 1975. Logic and conversation. In *Syntax and semantics*. Vol. 3. *Speech acts*, ed. P. Cole and J. L. Morgan, pp. 41–58. New York: Academic.

Grosz, B. J., and C. L. Sidner. 1986. Attention, intentions, and the structure of discourse. *Computational Liguistics and Computer Languages* 12: 175–204.

Guyotte, M. J., and R. J. Sternberg. 1981. A transitive-chain theory of syllogistic reasoning. *Cognitive Psychology* 13: 461–525.

Hall, R. P. 1989. Computational approaches to analogical reasoning: A comparative analysis. *Artificial Intelligence* 39: 39–120.

Hammond, K. 1986. The use of remindings in planning. *Proceedings Eighth Annual Conference of the Cognitive Science Society*, pp. 442–451. Amherst, MA.

Haugeland, J. 1981. Semantic engines: Introduction to mind design. In *Mind design: Philosophy, psychology, artificial intelligence*, ed. J. Haugeland. Cambridge, MA: MIT Press.

Hawkins, J., R. D. Pea, J. Glick, and S. Scribner. 1984. Merds that laugh don't like mushrooms: Evidence for deductive reasoning by preschoolers. *Developmental Psychology* 20: 584–594.

Hayes, P. J. 1977. In defence of logic. *Proceedings IJCAI-77*, pp. 559–565. Cambridge, MA.

Hayes-Roth, F. 1978. The role of partial and best matches in knowledge systems. In *Pattern-directed inference systems*, ed. D. A. Waterman and F. Hayes-Roth, pp. 557–576. New York: Academic Press.

Hayes-Roth, F., D. A. Waterman, and D. B. Lenat. 1983. *Building expert systems*. Reading, MA: Addison-Wesley.

Hergenrather, J. R., and M. Rabinowitz. 1991. Age-related differences in the organization of children's knowledge of illness. *Developmental Psychology* 27: 952–959.

Hesse, M. R. 1963. Models and analogies in science. In *Newman history and philosophy of science series 14*, ed. M. A. Hoskin. London: Sheed and Ward.

Hobbs, J. R. 1983a. Metaphor interpretation as selective inferencing: Cognitive processes in understanding metaphor (Part 1). *Empirical Studies of the Arts* 1: 17–33.

Hobbs, J. R. 1983b. Metaphor interpretation as selective inferencing: Cognitive processes in understanding metaphor (Part 2). *Empirical Studies of the Arts* 1: 125–142.

Hofstadter, D. 1984. The copycat project: An experiment in nondeterminism and creative analogies. AI Memo 755. Cambridge, MA: MIT Artificial Intelligence Laboratory.

Holyoak, K. J. 1985. The pragmatics of analogical transfer. *Psychological Learning and Motivation* 19: 59–87.

Holyoak, K. J., and K. Koh. 1987. Surface and structural similarity in analogical transfer. *Memory & Cognition* 15: 332–340.

Holyoak, K. J., and P. Thagard. 1989. A computational model of analogical problem solving. In *Similarity and analogical reasoning*, ed. S. Vosniadou and A. Ortony, pp. 242–266. Cambridge: Cambridge University Press.

Horgan, J. 1993, October. The death of proof. *Scientific American*, pp. 93–103.

Hovy, E. H. 1987. Some pragmatic decision criteria in generation. In *Natural language generation: New results in artificial intelligence*, ed. G. Kempen, pp. 3–19. Dordrecht, Netherlands: Kluwer Academic.

Hovy, E. H. 1988. Generating language with a phrasal lexicon. In *Natural language generation systems*, ed. D. D. McDonald and L. Bolo, pp. 353–384. New York: Springer.

Hovy, E. H. 1990. Pragmatics and natural language generation. *Artificial Intelligence* 43: 153–197.

Johnson-Laird, P. N., and M. Steedman. 1978. The psychology of syllogisms. *Cognitive Psychology* 10: 64–99.

Kaelbling, L. 1987. An architecture for intelligent reactive systems. In *Reasoning about action and plans: Proceedings of the 1986 workshop*, ed. M. P. Georgeff and A. L. Lansky. San Mateo, CA: Morgan Kaufmann.

Kahneman, D., and D. T. Miller. 1986. Norm theory: Comparing reality to its alternatives. *Psychological Review* 93: 136–153.

Kaplan, C. A., and H. A. Simon. 1990. In search of insight. *Cognitive Psychology* 22: 374–419.

Karmiloff-Smith, A. 1988. A child is a theoretician, not an inductivist. *Mind and Language* 3: 183–195.

Kedar-Cabelli, S. 1985. Purpose-directed analogy. *Proceedings Seventh Annual Conference of the Cognitive Science Society*, pp. 150–159. Irvine, CA.

Keil, F. C. 1981. Constraints on knowledge and cognitive development. *Psychological Review* 88: 197–227.

Kern, L. H., H. L. Mirels, and V. G. Hinshaw. 1983. Scientists' understanding of propositional logic: An experimental investigation. *Social Studies of Science* 13: 131–146.

Kirsh, D. 1990. When is information explicitly represented? In *Information, language, and cognition*, ed. P. Hanson. Vancouver: University of British Columbia Press.

Klahr, D. 1985. Solving problems with ambiguous subgoal ordering: Preschoolers' performance. *Child Development* 56: 940–952.

Klahr, D., and K. Dunbar. 1988. Dual space search during scientific reasoning. *Cognitive Science* 12: 1–55.

Klahr, D., K. Dunbar, and A. L. Fay. 1990. Designing good experiments to test "bad" hypotheses. In *Computational models of scientific discovery and theory formation*, ed. J. Shrager and P. Langley. San Mateo, CA: Morgan Kaufmann.

Klahr, D., A. L. Fay, and K. Dunbar. 1993. Heuristics for scientific experimentation: A developmental study. *Cognitive Psychology* 25: 111–146.

Klahr, D., and M. Robinson. 1981. Formal assessment of problem solving and planning processes in preschool children. *Cognitive Psychology* 13: 113–148.

Klayman, J., and Y. Ha. 1987. Confirmation, disconfirmation and information in hypothesis testing. *Psychological Review* 94: 211–228.

Kline, M. 1985. *Mathematics and the search for knowledge.* New York: Oxford University Press.

Kling, R. E. 1971. Reasoning by analogy with applications to heuristic problem solving: A case study. Ph.D. dissertation, Stanford University.

Kolodner, J. L. 1983. Maintaining organization in a dynamic long-term memory. *Cognitive Science* 7: 243–280.

Kolodner, J. L., and R. Simpson. 1988. The MEDIATOR: A case study of a case-based problem solver. Technical Report GIT-ICS-88/11. Atlanta: Georgia Institute of Technology, School of Information and Computer Science.

Kuhn, D., E. Amsel, and M. O'Loughlin. 1988. *The development of scientific thinking skills.* New York: Academic Press.

Lakoff, G., and M. Johnson. 1980. *Metaphors we live by.* Chicago: University of Chicago Press.

Lehnert, W. G. 1982. Plot units: A narrative summarization strategy. In *Strategies for natural language processing*, ed. W. G. Lehnert and M. H. Ringle, pp. 375–414. Hillsdale, NJ: Erlbaum.

Lenat, D. B., and E. A. Feigenbaum. 1991. On the thresholds of knowledge. *Artificial Intelligence* 47: 185–250.

Lenat, D. B., and R. V. Guha. 1988. *Building large knowledge-based systems: Representation and inference in the CYC project.* Reading, MA: Addison-Wesley.

Levesque, H. J. 1984. A logic of implicit and explicit belief. *Proceedings AAAI-84*, pp. 198–202. Austin, TX.

Malgady, R. G., and M. G. Johnson. 1980. Measurement of figurative language: Semantic feature models of comprehension and appreciation. In *Cognition and figurative language*, ed. R. P. Honeck and R. R. Hoffman, pp. 239–258. Hillsdale, NJ: Erlbaum.

Marcus, S. L., and L. J. Rips. 1979. Conditional reasoning. *Journal of Verbal Learning & Verbal Behavior* 18: 199–223.

Markman, E. M. 1979. Realizing that you don't understand: Elementary school children's awareness of inconsistencies. *Child Development* 50: 643–655.

Markovits, H. 1984. Awareness of the "possible" as a mediator of formal thinking in conditional reasoning problems. *British Journal of Psychology* 75: 367–376.

Markovits, H. In press. Reasoning with contrary-to-fact propositions. *Journal of Experimental Child Psychology*.

Markovits, H., and G. Nantel. 1989. The belief-bias effect in the production and evaluation of logical conclusions. *Memory & Cognition* 17: 11–17.

McCarthy, J. 1968. Programs with common sense. In *Semantic information processing*, ed. M. Minsky, pp. 403–410. Cambridge, MA: MIT Press.

McCarthy, J. 1979. Ascribing mental qualities to machines. Technical report STAN-CS-79-725, AIM-326. Stanford, CA: Stanford University, Department of Computer Science.

McCarthy, J. 1988. Mathematical logic in artificial intelligence. *Daedalus* 117: 297–311.

McDermott, D. V. 1981. Artificial intelligence meets natural stupidity. In *Mind design: Philosophy, psychology, artificial intelligence*, ed. J. Haugeland, pp. 143–160. Cambridge, MA: MIT Press.

McDermott, J. 1978. ANA: An assimilating and accommodating production system. Technical Report CMU-CS-78-156. Pittsburgh, PA: Carnegie-Mellon University, Computer Science Department.

McDermott, J. 1979. Learning to use analogies. *Proceedings IJCAI-79*, pp. 568–576. Tokyo, Japan.

Miller, G. A., C. Fellbaum, J. Kegl, and K. Miller. 1988. WORDNET: An electronic lexical reference system based on theories of lexical memory. *Revue Québécoise Linguistique* 17: 181–213.

Miller, G. A., and P. Johnson-Laird. 1976. *Language and perception.* Cambridge, MA: Harvard University Press.

Minsky, M. 1975. A framework for representing knowledge. In *The psychology of computer vision*, ed. P. H. Winston, pp. 211–277. New York: McGraw-Hill.

Mitroff, I. I. 1974. *The subjective side of science*. New York: Elsevier.

Munyer, J. C. 1981. Analogy as a means of discovery in problem solving and learning. Ph.D. dissertation, University of California at Santa Cruz.

Nagel, T. 1986. *The view from nowhere*. Oxford: Oxford University Press.

Newell, A. 1982. The knowledge level. *Artificial Intelligence* 19: 87–127.

Nilsson, N. J. 1991. Logic and artificial intelligence. *Artificial Intelligence* 47: 31–56.

Oakhill, J. V., and P. N. Johnson-Laird. 1985. The effects of belief on the spontaneous production of syllogistic conclusions. *Quarterly Journal of Experimental Psychology*, 37A: 553–569.

O'Brien, D. P., G. Costa, and W. F. Overton. 1986. Evaluations of causal and conditional hypotheses. *Quarterly Journal of Experimental Psychology* 38A: 493–512.

Palmer, S. E. 1989. Levels of description in information processing theories of analogy. In *Similarity and analogical reasoning*, ed. S. Vosniadou and A. Ortony, pp. 332–345. Cambridge: Cambridge University Press.

Pirolli, P. L., and J. R. Anderson. 1985. The role of learning from examples in the acquisition of recursive programming skills. *Canadian Journal of Psychology* 39: 240–272.

Raibert, M. H. 1986. Legged robots. *Communications of the ACM* 29: 499–514.

Raibert, M. H., and I. E. Sutherland. 1983, January. Machines that walk. *Scientific American*, pp. 44–53.

Rattermann, M., and D. Gentner. 1987. Analogy and similarity: Determinants of accessibility and inferential soundness. *Proceedings Ninth Annual Meeting of the Cognitive Science Society*, pp. 23–34. Seattle, WA.

Revlin, R., and V. Leirer. 1978. The effects of personal biases on syllogistic reasoning: Rational decisions from personalized representations. In *Human reasoning*, ed. R. Revlin and R. E. Meyer, pp. 51–82. Washington, DC: Winston-Wiley.

Revlin, R., V. Leirer, H. Yopp, and R. Yopp. 1980. The belief-bias effect in formal reasoning: The influence of knowledge on logic. *Memory & Cognition* 8: 584–592.

Rosenschein, S. J., and L. P. Kaelbling. 1987. The synthesis of machines with provable epistemic properties. In *Proceedings of the 1986 conference on theoretical aspects of reasoning about knowledge*, ed. J. Y. Halpern, pp. 83–98. San Mateo, CA: Morgan Kaufmann.

Ross, B. H. 1984. Remindings and their effects in learning a cognitive skill. *Cognitive Psychology* 16: 371–416.

Ross, B. H. 1987. This is like that: The use of earlier problems and the separation of similarity effects. *Journal of Experimental Psychology: Learning, Memory and Cognition* 13: 371–416.

Ross, B. H. 1989. Distinguishing types of superficial similarities: Different effects on the access and use of earlier problems. *Journal of Experimental Psychology: Learning, Memory and Cognition* 15: 456–468.

Schank, R. C. 1972. "Semantics" in conceptual analysis. *Lingua* 30: 101–140.

Schank, R. C. 1975. *Conceptual information processing.* Amsterdam: North-Holland.

Schank, R. C. 1982. *Dynamic memory: A theory of reminding and learning in computers and people.* London: Cambridge University Press.

Schank, R. C., and R. P. Abelson. 1977. *Scripts, Plans, Goals and Understanding.* Hillsdale, NJ: Erlbaum.

Schauble, L. 1990. Belief revision in children: The role of prior knowledge and strategies for generating evidence. *Journal of Experimental Child Psychology* 49: 31–57.

Searle, J. R. 1969. *Speech acts.* New York: Cambridge University Press.

Searle, J. R. 1981. Minds, brains, and programs. *The Behavioral and Brain Sciences* 3: 417–424.

Seifert, C., G. McKoon, R. Abelson, and R. Ratcliff. 1986. Memory connections between thematically similar episodes. *Journal of Experimental Psychology: Learning, Memory and Cognition* 12: 220–231.

Shrager, J. 1987. Theory change via view application instructionless learning. *Machine Learning* 2: 247–276.

Siegler, R. S., and R. M. Liebert. 1975. Acquisition of formal scientific reasoning by 10- and 13-year-olds: Designing a factorial experiment. *Developmental Psychology* 10: 401–402.

Simon, H. A. 1977. *Models of discovery.* Dordrecht, Netherlands: D. Reidel.

Simpson, R. L. 1985. A computer model of case-based reasoning in problem solving: An investigation in the domain of dispute mediation. Ph.D. dissertation, Georgia Institute of Technology.

Smith, B. C. In press. *A view from somewhere: An essay on the foundations of computation and intentionality.* Cambridge, MA: MIT Press/Bradford Books.

Smith, B. C. 1991. The owl and the electric encyclopedia. *Artificial Intelligence* 47: 251–288.

Smolensky, P. 1988. On the proper treatment of connectionism. *The Behavioral and Brain Sciences* 11: 1–74.

Sodian, B., D. Zaitchik, and S. Carey. 1991. Young children's differentiation of hypothetical beliefs from evidence. *Child Development* 62: 753–766.

Spencer, R. M., and R. W. Weisberg. 1986. Context-dependent effects on analogical transfer. *Memory & Cognition* 14: 442–449.

Sternberg, R. J. 1977. *Intelligence, information processing and analogical reasoning: The componential analysis of human abilities.* Hillsdale, NJ: Erlbaum.

Suchman, L. A. 1986. *Plans and situated actions*. Cambridge, MA: Cambridge University Press.

Thagard, P. 1988. *Computational philosophy of science*. Cambridge, MA: MIT Press/Bradford Books.

Thagard, P. 1989. Explanatory coherence. *The Behavioral and Brain Sciences* 12: 435–467.

Thagard, P., D. Cohen, and K. J. Holyoak. 1989. Chemical analogies: Two kinds of explanation. *Proceedings IJCAI-89*, pp. 819–824. Detroit, MI.

Thagard, P., K. J. Holyoak, G. Nelson, and D. Gochfeld. 1990. Analog retrieval by constraint satisfaction. *Artificial Intelligence* 46: 259–310.

Tschirgi, J. E. 1980. Sensible reasoning: A hypothesis about hypotheses. *Child Development* 51: 1–10.

Tumblin, A., and B. Gholson. 1981. Hypothesis theory and the development of conceptual learning. *Psychological Bulletin* 90: 102–124.

Vosniadou, S., and W. F. Brewer. 1992. Mental models of the earth: A study of conceptual change in childhood. *Cognitive Psychology* 24: 535–585.

Wagman, M. 1980a. PLATO DCS, an interactive computer system for personal counseling. *Journal of Counseling Psychology* 27: 16–30.

Wagman, M. 1984. *The dilemma and the computer: Theory, research, and applications to counseling psychology*. New York: Praeger.

Wagman, M. 1988. *Computer Psychotherapy Systems: Theory and Research Foundations*. New York: Praeger.

Wagman, M. 1993. *Cognitive psychology and artificial intelligence: Theory and research in cognitive science*. Westport, CT: Praeger.

Wagman, M., and K. W. Kerber. 1980. PLATO DCS, an interactive computer system for personal counseling: Technical description and performance data. *JSAS Catalog of Selected Documents in Psychology* 9, 20, MS 1827.

Wason, P. C. 1968. Reasoning about a rule. *Quarterly Journal of Experimental Psychology* 20: 273–281.

Wilson, M. D., ed. 1969. *The essential Descartes*. New York: Mentor.

Winograd, T. 1975. Frame representations and the declarative/procedural controversy. In *Representation and understanding: Studies in cognitive science*, ed. D. Bobrow and A. Collins, pp. 185–210. New York: Academic Press.

Winograd, T., and F. Flores. 1986. *Understanding computers and cognition: A new foundation for design*. Norwood, NJ: Ablex.

Winston, P. H. 1975. Learning structural descriptions from examples. In *The psychology of computer vision*, ed. P. H. Winston. New York: McGraw-Hill.

Winston, P. H. 1978. Learning by creating and justifying transfer frames. *Artificial Intelligence* 10: 147–172.

Winston, P. H. 1980. Learning and reasoning by analogy. *Communications of the ACM* 23: 689–703.

Winston, P. H. 1982. Learning new principles from precedents and exercises. *Artificial Intelligence* 19: 321–350.

Winston, P. H. 1983. Learning by augmenting rules and accumulating censors. *Proceedings International Machine Learning Workshop*, pp. 2–11. Monticello, IL.

Winston, P. H. 1984. *Artificial intelligence*. Reading, MA: Addison-Wesley.

Winston, P. H. 1986. Learning by augmenting rules and accumulating censors. In *Machine learning: An artificial intelligence approach*, ed. R. S. Michalski, J. G. Carbonell, and T. M. Mitchell, pp. 45–61. Los Altos, CA: Morgan Kaufmann.

Winston, P. H., T. O. Binford, B. Katz, and M. Lowry. 1983. Learning physical descriptions from functional definitions. *Proceedings AAAI-83*, pp. 433–439. Washington, DC.

Wiser, M. 1989. Does learning science involve theory change? Paper presented at the Biannual Meeting of the Society for Research in Child Development, Kansas City, April 30.

Wisniewski, E. H., and D. L. Medin. 1991. Harpoons and long sticks: The interaction of theory and similarity in rule induction. In *Concept formation: Knowledge and experience in unsupervised learning*, ed. D. H. Fisher, Jr., M. H. Pazzani, and P. Langley. San Mateo, CA: Morgan Kaufmann.

Woodworth, R. S., and S. B. Sells. 1935. An atmosphere effect in syllogistic reasoning. *Journal of Experimental Psychology* 18: 451–460.

Author Index

Subject Index

ABOUT THE AUTHOR

MORTON WAGMAN is Professor Emeritus of Psychology at the University of Illinois at Urbana-Champaign and is a Diplomate in Counseling Psychology, American Board of Professional Psychology. He was honored as Distinguished Psychologist by the American Psychological Association in 1990. His most recent books include: *The General Unified Theory of Intelligence* (1997), *Human Intellect and Cognitive Science* (1996), *The Sciences of Cognition* (1995), *Cognitive Psychology and Artificial Intelligence* (1993), *Cognitive Science and Concepts of Mind* (1991), *Artificial Intelligence and Human Cognition* (1991), and *The Dilemma and the Computer* (1984), all published by Praeger.

ISBN 0-275-95853-1

90000>

EAN

HARDCOVER BAR CODE